DEVELOPED BY THE ROYAL YACHTING

Onboard Weather Handbook

Understanding and Predicting Conditions at Sea

Chris Tibbs

International Marine / McGraw-Hill

Camden, Maine • New York • Chicago • San Francisco
Lisbon • London • Madrid • Mexico City • Milan • New Delhi
San Juan • Seoul • Singapore • Sydney • Toronto

The McGraw·Hill Companies

1 2 3 4 5 6 7 8 9 RRDSHEN 0 9 8

© 2008 Royal Yachting Association.
First published in the United Kingdom 2005 as *RYA Weather Handbook,* Second Edition.

Library of Congress Cataloging-in-Publication Data
Tibbs, Chris.
   Onboard weather handbook : understanding and predicting conditions at sea / Chris Tibbs.
          p. cm.
      Includes index.
      Rev. ed. of: RYA weather handbook, Northern Hemisphere.
      ISBN-13: 978-0-07-149715-2 (pbk. : alk. paper)
   1. Marine meteorology—Handbooks, manuals, etc.   2. Weather forecasting—Handbooks, manuals, etc.   3. Aids to navigation—Handbooks, manuals, etc.   I. Tibbs, Chris. RYA weather handbook, Northern Hemisphere.   II. Title.
      QC993.84.T53 2008
      551.65162—dc22   2007046233

ISBN 978-0-07-149715-2
MHID 0-07-149715-3

Questions regarding the content of this book should be addressed to

International Marine
P.O. Box 220
Camden, ME 04843
www.internationalmarine.com

Questions regarding the ordering of this book should be addressed to

The McGraw-Hill Companies
Customer Service Department
P.O. Box 547
Blacklick, OH 43004
Retail customers: 1-800-262-4729
Bookstores: 1-800-722-4726

Illustrations by Sarah Selman except where noted.
Title page photo by NOAA. Chapter opener photos by Gary John Norman/Bluegreen Pictures; side tab photo by Chris Tibbs.

Contents

1 Introduction 1

2 Weather Theory 4

3 Synoptic Weather Charts 10

4 Clouds 14

5 Lows 21

6 High-Pressure Systems 45

7 Predicting the Wind from Weather Charts 49

8 Land's Effect on the Wind 58

9 Weather at Sea 73

10 Meteorological Dangers 77

11 **Hurricanes**   **91**

12 **Putting It All Together**   **98**

13 **Sailing Areas of North America**   **118**

14 **Around the World**   **128**

15 **Climate Change**   **136**

Weather Briefing Packages   **141**

Weather Websites   **146**

Glossary   **147**

A Note about Units   **151**

Index   **152**

CHAPTER 1

Introduction

The weather affects our sport like nothing else does. It can turn a pleasant trip into a battle, or vice versa.

Bad weather means different things to different people, depending on the size of their boats, their general level of experience, and their perceptions of what is a good sail and what is a bad one.

Weather forecasts help us harness the *wind* to our best advantage and to avoid hazards.

Becoming a competent weather forecaster takes a lifetime of training and experience, but no matter how good anyone becomes, computer-generated weather models will always outperform people in predicting large-scale weather patterns. It is better to concentrate on interpreting these forecasts for your area, modifying them for local conditions, and by adding observations, improving their accuracy over a short period of time. This book is therefore not intended to replace broadcast forecasts but to add to our understanding of the weather.

Weather can be split up into seven variables, all of which are linked, and all of which affect our sailing. For sailors, the most obvious conditions are probably the wind and visibility, but these are linked to *precipitation*, clouds, temperature, and *humidity*. They are all linked to the atmospheric *pressure* and the general *synoptic* situation.

None of these variables should be looked at in isolation; although we are normally interested in only a small geographical area, we have to look at the larger picture before we can refine our forecast to our particular area.

At the synoptic scale, meteorologists are concerned with large systems of *high* and *low pressure*, and with *air masses* that may cover many thousands of square miles. This broadbrush picture is often portrayed by a synoptic chart or weather map, showing the meteorological features overlaid onto a geographical base map. (See below and Chapter 3 for more on synoptic scale weather maps.)

An analysis chart is based on actual observations and measurements at a specific time. From it, meteorologists can produce predicted or forecast charts, which give a general idea of how conditions are likely to change over a wide area.

It is these that are summarized by the general synopsis section of a marine forecast.

Armed with the synoptic overview, we can look at a smaller area—the area in which we will be sailing over the next few days, perhaps. This is *mesoscale* meteorology—dealing with areas of a few hundred square miles at a time, or about the size of an individual zone in an offshore waters forecast. Mesoscale forecasts usually give a reasonable indication of the average conditions across the whole area. Bear in mind, though, that there can be a big difference between, for instance, conditions offshore of North Florida and the South Bahamas, even though they are both within the southwest North Atlantic zone.

What is usually of most interest to the sailor is the local weather, particularly over the relatively short term. Coastal waters forecasts cover this to a certain extent, but they deal with quite long sections of coast: these forecasts may not give enough detail to tell us how conditions will change as we round the next headland in half an hour, or to help pick the best spot to anchor within a harbor.

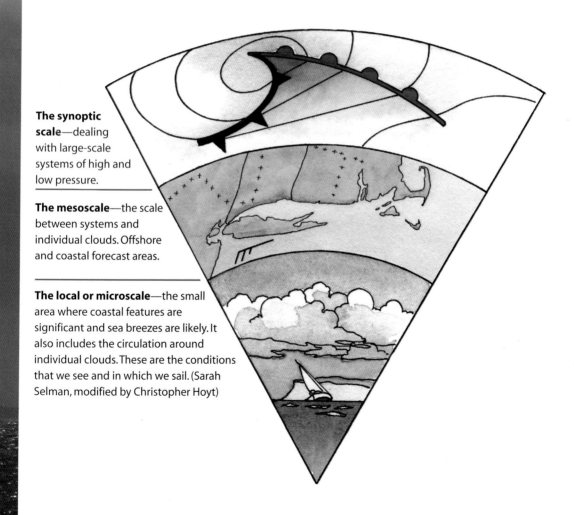

The synoptic scale—dealing with large-scale systems of high and low pressure.

The mesoscale—the scale between systems and individual clouds. Offshore and coastal forecast areas.

The local or microscale—the small area where coastal features are significant and sea breezes are likely. It also includes the circulation around individual clouds. These are the conditions that we see and in which we sail. (Sarah Selman, modified by Christopher Hoyt)

Safety, of course, is paramount; although there is always the risk of getting caught out by bad weather, an important feature of onboard weather forecasting is that it can help us recognize, well in advance, if a situation is likely to become marginal—or worse!

This book starts with weather theory and looks at the global circulation of air, then concentrates on progressively smaller areas down to micrometeorology and the circulation of air around clouds.

The behavior of the wind and weather around coastlines is important, because the land affects the weather in a variety of ways: There is a thermal effect caused by the changing temperature, for instance, as well as a mechanical effect caused by the topography. These can make a significant difference in the wind's direction and strength, but their effects are often so localized that they are not included in the forecast.

Bad weather in North America and most places around the world is generally from *depressions* (lows), so a lot of emphasis is placed on how lows develop and how they are structured. (See Chapter 5.) By understanding this structure and movement, we can gain a greater understanding of how they will affect us.

Meteorological Terms

While jargon has been kept to a minimum, some meteorological terms are necessary as they have precise meanings and are well worth remembering. At their first use, they are italicized; you will find definitions for these italicized terms in the glossary in the back of the book.

Red sky at night sailor's delight, red sky in morning sailors take warning. These pictures were taken six hours apart ahead of an approaching depression. The rising sun is reflected by the invading clouds. (Chris Tibbs)

CHAPTER 2

Weather Theory

Climate *is an average of the weather conditions, while* **weather** *is the day-to-day variability. In other words, we look at the climate to decide which boat to buy and what sails to equip it with, but we look at the weather to tell us the size of headsail and how many reefs to put in on a particular day.*

HEAT AND GLOBAL CIRCULATION

The single most important factor that drives the movement of air and thus controls our weather and climate is heat. The sun heats the earth's surface, be it land or water, and that surface heats the air above it.

This principle is fundamental in understanding the weather. The air's temperature falls as we go up through the atmosphere to a region called the *tropopause*. The tropopause is found at an altitude of about 40,000 feet (12km)—higher in the tropics and lower at the poles. It is in this lowest area of the atmosphere that all our weather occurs, and in which weather systems grow and decline. We sail in only the very bottom layer, but the vertical structure is important in understanding the weather.

Moisture is also important in global circulation. The warmer the air the more moisture it can hold, but as moisture evaporates and condenses, *latent heat* is absorbed and released. Moisture, therefore, plays its part in moving energy around in the form of heat and latent heat. Surprisingly, moist air is more buoyant than dry air, so it also contributes to the vertical movements that are so important in creating weather.

The equatorial regions of the globe are strongly heated by the sun. This heat is transported poleward by global air circulation, and to a lesser extent by ocean currents. This dispersal of heat toward the poles helps to regulate the earth's temperature. As the sea itself has a huge heat capacity it also acts as a regulator, moderating temperatures along coastal regions of the world, while extreme temperatures are to be found inland near the centers of large landmasses.

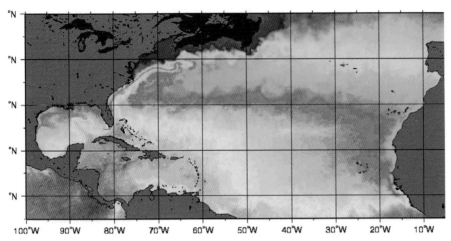

The Gulf Stream and North Atlantic Drift bring warm water northward. Red denotes warmest water and blue coldest.

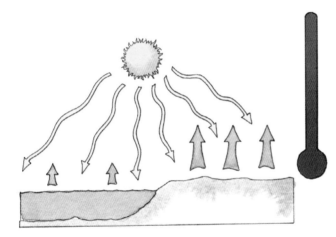

The sun heats the land quickly and this heat is released into the air. The land also cools quickly at night. The sea is slower to heat and cool, remaining at a more constant temperature throughout the day.

As the surface temperature increases at the equator it heats the air above. The warm air rises and expands, which lowers the air pressure at the surface. Air pressure can be thought of as the weight of air vertically above us, so as the air heats, rises, and expands, the pressure lowers. The rising air reaches the tropopause and spreads out, moving toward the poles. This is a little like a bonfire; the heat and smoke of a bonfire rises to be replaced by cooler air coming in from the side creating circulation, but in this case it all happens on a global scale. We see this rising and overturning air on many scales in weather forecasting, from the global to circulation under a convective cloud.

The warm air that is spreading out aloft slowly cools as it moves poleward, causing it to sink and adding to the column of air already there. Thus the air pressure at the surface increases and we get an area of high pressure. The surface air under the higher pressure is moved away—squeezed out—and heads toward low pressure.

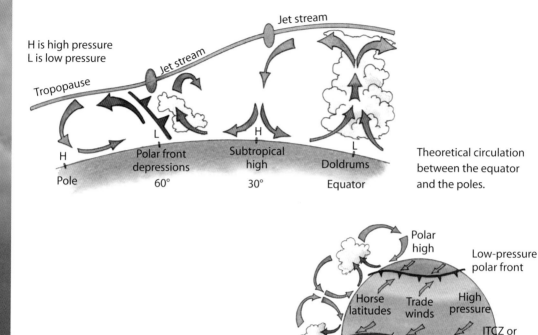

H is high pressure
L is low pressure

Theoretical circulation between the equator and the poles.

Idealized global circulation.

Two more fundamentals of weather and systems are illustrated here: Surface air moves from high to low pressure, and air in low pressure rises. The opposite happens in high pressure, i.e., air descends and moves away from the center at the surface.

This generates the world's main wind patterns and would all be very neat and uniform if it were not for the uneven distribution of land, and the effect the spinning earth has on our lives. The spinning earth causes the wind around lows in the Northern Hemisphere to circulate counterclockwise and to circulate clockwise around high pressure. The directions are reversed in the Southern Hemisphere. More about this in Chapter 14.

AIR MASSES

Because the air spends long periods of time over land or sea it takes on certain characteristics, such as temperature and humidity. Air over cold land, for instance, cools and is relatively dry. Over a warm sea however it becomes warm and moist. We have already learned that the warmer the air, the more moisture it can hold before it becomes saturated. This is particularly relevant for sailors on coasts where the prevailing wind brings air that has spent a long time over the oceans.

The air from any particular region has very small differences in temperature or humidity over an area spanning hundreds or even thousands of miles. This is important for us as these characteristics define what the weather conditions are likely to be within that air mass.

The accompanying illustration shows where North America's different air masses come from and gives the main characteristics.

The origin of the air gives it its characteristics and the track that the air takes will modify those characteristics. As a rule, the temperature of the surface that the air is moving over will either heat or cool the air mass from below. This will make it either more or less stable.

The importance of where the air has spent its time recently becomes obvious when looking at lows. In the warm sector, the moist tropical maritime air brings low cloud cover and *drizzle* to exposed coasts. In the spring, *fog* forms over the cool sea which will persist until the air mass changes.

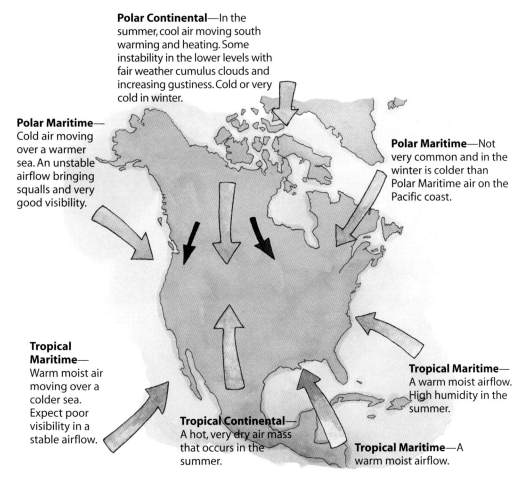

Polar Continental—In the summer, cool air moving south warming and heating. Some instability in the lower levels with fair weather cumulus clouds and increasing gustiness. Cold or very cold in winter.

Polar Maritime—Cold air moving over a warmer sea. An unstable airflow bringing squalls and very good visibility.

Polar Maritime—Not very common and in the winter is colder than Polar Maritime air on the Pacific coast.

Tropical Maritime—Warm moist air moving over a colder sea. Expect poor visibility in a stable airflow.

Tropical Continental—A hot, very dry air mass that occurs in the summer.

Tropical Maritime—A warm moist airflow. High humidity in the summer.

Tropical Maritime—A warm moist airflow.

A generalized view of the major North American air masses and their chacteristics. (Christopher Hoyt)

Unstable air mass after a *cold front* has passed. (Chris Tibbs)

Stable air mass with fog and *mist* in tropical maritime air. (Helen Tibbs)

Air masses move, but when they meet each other they don't usually mix very readily. This means that where two air masses meet, there are likely to be sharp changes in temperature and humidity. These meetings of air masses are described as *fronts*.

The most dramatic change in air mass that we see is when a cold front passes. First there is drizzle then heavy rain, then the sky clears giving good visibility, then a noticeable drop in temperature, and at times rain squalls.

Atmospheric Stability

Unstable	Stable
Big vertical movement in the atmosphere giving heaped clouds and gusty conditions.	Little vertical movement in the atmosphere, giving flat layers of clouds.
Typical of cold air moving over a warm surface.	Typical of warm air moving over a cold surface.

LOW PRESSURE AND THE POLAR FRONT

The weather that dominates most mid-latitude regions both north and south of the equator is caused by the procession of low-pressure systems that arrive from the west.

There are preferred locations where *cyclogenesis* (the creation of lows) most often occur; for North America this includes the Gulf of Alaska and North Pacific, the eastern slopes of the Rockies, the Great Basin, the Gulf of Mexico, and the Atlantic Ocean east of the Carolinas. Once developed, the usual track of mid-latitude *cyclones* is to the east or the northeast.

Near Cape Hatteras, where the *Gulf Stream* brings energy north in the form of heat and moisture, cyclogenesis can happen rapidly, creating quickly deteriorating conditions. This has given the Cape Hatteras area a well-deserved fearsome reputation.

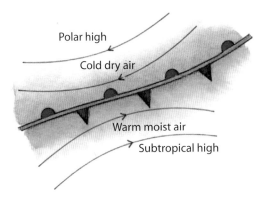

The polar front in equilibrium.

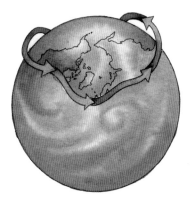

The polar front *jet stream*, often referred to as simply the jet stream, is situated between warm and cold air masses and follows a generally west to east direction.

The majority of these lows form along what are known as the *polar fronts* (as shown in the global circulation diagram on page 6). This is where the air circulating around the subtropical high meets the colder air flowing in the opposite direction.

These two air masses meet but do not mix and a small disturbance on this polar front causes a low to form. The spinning earth forces this air to rotate counterclockwise in the Northern Hemisphere and a low-pressure system is born (see Chapter 5).

The air masses retain their original characteristics and do not mix with each other, leaving a distinct dividing line between them, called a front, like the front line between opposing armies. Interestingly, this idea of the weather systems was devised by the Norwegians during the First World War and is still in use today. The concept of armies fighting along fronts was easily transferred to the weather where large temperature and humidity differences "fight it out."

Although this model is sometimes a long way from reality, it is useful to illustrate what happens. It must, however, be used with some caution as the weather does not always conform and no two lows are ever identical.

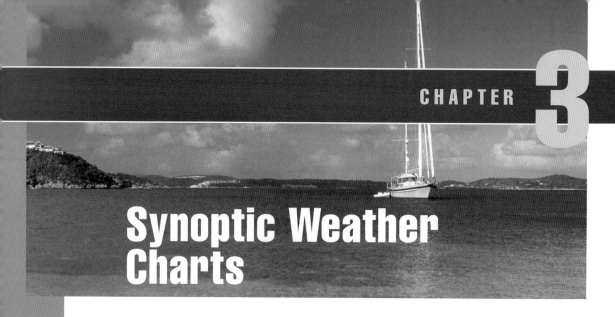

CHAPTER 3

Synoptic Weather Charts

Representing the weather on a flat piece of paper is similar to representing the land's contours on a topographic map.

The main variable on a weather chart is the surface pressure. This is measured in *millibars* (mb) and is represented on a synoptic chart by lines called *isobars*. Millibars are used in almost all marine weather forecasts both nationally and internationally. (Some charts found on the Internet and in Europe may be shown in hectopascals, which are interchangeable with millibars.) Older *barometers* may be calibrated in inches of mercury while many new ones have both scales on the dial.

In discussing air pressure, we are generally concerned with conditions at the surface of the earth. Synoptic charts, which show surface air pressure, are the most readily available type, and the most useful for boaters. These charts are the subject of the following discussion. The use of upper-air, or high altitude, charts is discussed separately in Chapter 12.

Like contours on a topographic map joining places of the same height, isobars join places recording the same pressure. Low pressure is like a valley, and high pressure is like hills and mountains. Even some of the jargon is the same, with ridges and cols (the lowest point of a ridge or saddle between two peaks) around the mountains of the high while *troughs* extend from lows.

The analogy can be taken one step further with the wind moving from high to low pressure just as gravity would move an object on the land. Here, though, the similarities end as the rotation of the earth takes control and bends the surface wind to make it follow the isobars with only a few degrees of outflow from highs, and inward flow to lows.

On a land map, the closer together the contours the steeper the slope of the hill. On a weather chart, the closer together the isobars the greater the *pressure gradient* and the stronger the wind. This is important when interpreting weather maps as there is a direct relationship between the pressure gradient and the wind speed. We will look at measuring the wind speed from a chart in Chapter 7 and see how to adjust it to get our sailing wind.

We sail in what is known meteorologically as the *boundary layer*—the air closest to the earth's surface (see page 12). This is where most of the interaction between the surface and atmosphere occurs.

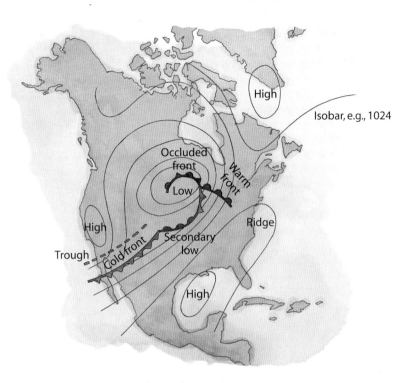

A generalized synoptic weather chart. (Christopher Hoyt)

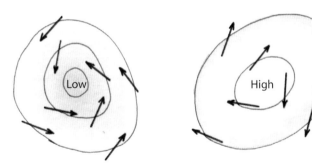

Circulation around low and high pressure in the Northern Hemisphere. The surface wind is in toward the center of the low (left) and out of a high (right).

The surface has a profound effect on the boundary layer so what happens close to the surface can be quite different from what happens much higher up. There is no strict height definition for the boundary layer; its extent varies with conditions but for working purposes we can use 2,000 feet (600 meters).

Although the weather maps we use are for the surface, in reality they are giving us information about the wind at the top of the boundary layer. This has to be modified to be of real use to us.

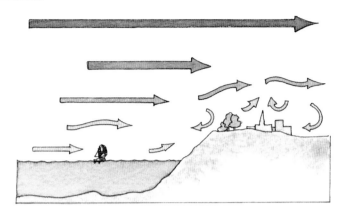

We sail in the boundary layer where drag and turbulence are found. The more obstructions to the wind there are, the rougher the surface is.

Above the boundary layer, the wind follows the isobars and runs parallel to them. It is also convenient to measure the wind's strength by measuring the distance between isobars and hence the gradient of the wind. The standard isobar spacing is 4mb—but do check, as some charts found on the Internet will have 5mb spacing and others 2mb.

Isobars

The closer together the isobars are on a synoptic chart, the steeper the pressure gradient and the stronger the wind. (See Chapter 7.)

A Note about Units

Meteorology has a mixture of units that have developed over the years. Different branches have their favorite units and although research uses the more scientific SI units, practical meteorologists have stuck with more traditional ones.

This has led to an odd mixture of units. It is not uncommon to have cloud heights described in feet or thousands of feet, visibility in meters, and wind speed in knots—all within one forecast!

Pressure is generally given in millibars (mb) or hectopascals (hPa); 1mb is equal to 1hPa so these units are interchangable. Older barometers and some newspaper weather maps may still show pressure in inches or millimeters of mercury. (To convert inches of mercury to millibars, multiply by 33.86. To convert millimeters of mercury to millibars, multiply by 1.33.)

The *knot* is the most common unit for wind speed, but some countries, particularly Scandinavia, are likely to give wind speed in meters per second (multiply meters per second by 2 to get an approximation in knots), while land forecasts will give wind speed in miles per hour or kilometers per hour in Canadian forecasts.

To sum it all up (see also A Note about Units, page 151):

1 knot = 1.15 mph = 1.85 kph = 0.514 meters/second.

Synoptic Chart Symbols

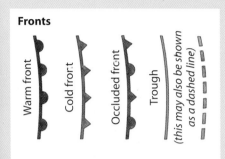

Fronts

Warm front · Cold front · Occluded front · Trough *(this may also be shown as a dashed line)*

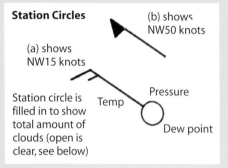

Station Circles

(a) shows NW15 knots

(b) shows NW50 knots

Station circle is filled in to show total amount of clouds (open is clear, see below)

Temp · Pressure · Dew point

Some charts have station circles showing the data recorded at the weather stations concerned.

The most useful information for sailors is in the form of a wind arrow attached to the circle, where each full barb represents 10 knots, and a half barb is 5 knots. The wind blows from the barbs to the center of the circle; the bottom half of this figure (a) shows the wind blowing from the northwest at 15 knots. If the barbs are replaced by a solid triangle, as in the top half of the figure (b), it represents 50 knots. Wind arrows may be shown on their own without a circle.

Other information may be found around a station circle in the positions shown in the figure. Additionally, the circle itself may be filled in to show the extent of the cloud cover, using the configurations shown below.

Other Common Symbols and Their Meanings

- ● Rain
- ❯ Drizzle
- ▽ Shower
- ✳ Snow
- △ Hail
- ⦦ Thunderstorm
- ▽ Squall
- ≡ Fog
- = Mist
- ∞ Haze

Station Circles Filled Denoting Cloud Cover

Clear · 1/8 · 2/8 · 3/8 · 4/8

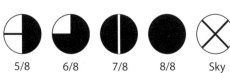

5/8 · 6/8 · 7/8 · 8/8 · Sky obscured

CHAPTER 4

Clouds

*On all but the clearest days there are clouds above our heads.
These clouds hold messages. With a bit of practice, we can begin
to understand why the clouds are there, what they are telling us,
and how to use their messages to our advantage.*

While the wind in our faces is an indication of horizontal air movement at the earth's surface, the clouds give a visual indication of what is happening overhead. They show the vertical profile of the weather, giving a three-dimensional picture of the atmosphere's movement.

The clouds' tracks across the sky show the direction of upper-level winds. Good examples of this are cirrus clouds (very high and wispy clouds sometimes referred to as *mares tails*) invading the sky from the west while the surface wind is southerly. These are a sure, and usually the first, sign of an approaching low. This is sometimes referred to as the "crosswind rule": when facing into the wind, if the upper clouds are approaching from the right the weather will deteriorate. The opposite is also usually true. Low clouds or *scud* (small fragmented low cloud) moving quickly may indicate a strong wind to come or that the wind is strong out at sea.

> Clouds are formed by air lifting and cooling until the *dew point* is reached and the water condenses and becomes visible.

Not only can we look upward to see the bottoms of clouds, we can also view satellite images to see the tops of clouds. With a bit of knowledge we can then take an educated guess at what is happening in between.

On a synoptic scale, clouds will tell us where we are within the system; on the local scale, clouds indicate gustiness and wind shifts.

Weather (synoptic) charts will give us an idea of what should be up there, but often there is such a jumble of clouds at different levels and of differing shapes and colors that it is tempting to give up and just say "it is cloudy." Although there are dozens of classifications and subdivisions to describe what we see, clouds can also be divided into much simpler, more general groups based on appearance and height.

CLOUD TYPES

The main three cloud types are **cumulus** (a heaped or lumpy cloud), **stratus** (layers of flat clouds), and **cirrus** (high wispy clouds). By adding a height characteristic of cirro for high clouds and **alto** for medium levels, we have our main classifications. One extra addition, **nimbus**, is for when the cloud is bearing rain (or snow)—whether it is actually raining or just looks as if it may do so soon. Cumulonimbus, for instance, is a heaped rain cloud, while nimbostratus means that rain is currently falling from thick layer clouds.

Judging the height of clouds is difficult even for a trained observer. It becomes easier with practice, especially when they are seen in the context of a large-scale system. Cumulus tends to be hard to define by height; although the base is low, the vertical extent may be 30,000 feet (as in the case of cumulonimbus clouds). The classification is therefore determined by the height of the base.

Mackerel sky: cirrocumulus and altocumulus clouds. (Chris Tibbs)

Altostratus clouds. (Chris Tibbs)

Types of Clouds

	Name	Abbreviation	Height Band
High layer	Cirrus—wispy, hair-like	Ci	Above 16,500ft (5,000m)
	Cirrostratus—fine layer, possible halo	Cs	
	Cirrocumulus—lumpy layer	Cc	
Medium layer	Altostratus—thin layer	As	6,500ft–16,500ft (2,000–5,000m)
	Altocumulus—lumpy layer	Ac	
Low layer	Stratus—uniform layer	St	Surface to 6,500ft (0–2,000m)
	Stratocumulus—undulating or lumpy layer	Sc	
	Nimbostratus—thick rain-bearing layer	Ns	
	Cumulus	Cu	From low level to tropopause— approx. 38,000ft (12km)
	Cumulonimbus	Cb	

Note: Cloud heights are traditionally given in feet and reports are usually given in feet or thousands of feet. Approximate heights are given as a guide only; clouds may extend through the bands and it is impossible to measure the height accurately by eye. In meteorological reports, cloud cover is given in oktas, or eighths, with 8/8 signifying an overcast sky (see page 13).

A cumulus cloud and its circulation. (Helen Tibbs photo)

EXTENSIVE LAYER CLOUDS

Extensive layer clouds form when there is large-scale ascent, mainly in lows and around fronts. This explains the cloud structure ahead of a *warm front* when warm, moist air is lifted over colder air (see the section Anatomy of a Low on pages 28–29). Large-scale or mass ascent also occurs when air is lifted over the land. This is called *orographic uplift* and is often visible when sailing near high coasts.

HEAPED OR CUMULUS CLOUDS

Heaped or cumulus clouds are formed by *convection*. Air and moisture are heated and rise from the surface forming a local thermal. To remain in equilibrium the air that rises must be replaced, giving a continuous local circulation.

This produces individual clouds that tend to form in lanes across the sky but there are clear patches where the cold air returns to the surface. Cumulus and their big brothers, cumulonimbus clouds, by their very nature generate this local air circulation that is so important to us when sailing (see Thunderstorms on pages 79–82).

ATMOSPHERIC STABILITY

Of all the messages that the clouds are giving us, one of the most important for sailing is about the stability of the atmosphere. We all know that hot air rises. If the rising warm air is lifted into relatively cooler air it will keep on rising, and clouds of great vertical extent are formed—towering cumulus or cumulonimbus. If the air above is relatively warm, however, there will be little vertical movement, and layer clouds will develop.

Therefore, big cumulus clouds are an indication of instability; we can expect *gusty* conditions, *showers*, and possibly squalls. Layer clouds show stability, giving fewer and lower gusts, and any increase in the wind speed is likely to be gradual.

Banner cloud. (Chris Tibbs)

These indicators of stability or instability will also tell us where we are within a forecast system—and the likely air mass we are in—allowing us to make better decisions in both the short and long term.

MARKING LANDFALLS

Cumulus clouds are often triggered by land or hills in the path of the airflow. It is common to see a cumulus cloud sitting on top of a high island.

If the airflow is stable, clouds may also mark a landfall with a banner cloud over the high land. In both cases the cloud over the land can be seen well before the land itself and has been a great indicator for mariners since boats first sailed beyond the sight of land.

RAIN

Apart from making us wet and correspondingly miserable, rain has significant effects on sailing and can tell us a lot about the weather. Heavy rain seriously reduces visibility and rain squalls bring strong gusts. The intensity of the rain is also an indication of where we are situated within a low. We'll look at this in greater detail when we look at the anatomy of a low and its life cycle in Chapter 5.

An interesting point, and one that helps in understanding forecasts, is that irrespective of how long the rain lasts, showers only come from convective clouds, i.e., cumulus and cumulonimbus.

For short bursts of rain from layer clouds, expected to last less than one hour, the term "intermittent" rain is used (and "continuous" if it were expected to last for over an hour). These labels may seem fussy, but they do help to describe the rain, and give a good indication of where we might be within a low.

Clouds

■ show the stability of the atmosphere

■ show where we are in a system

■ can be the first indication of approaching lows

■ indicate short-term changes in the wind

■ indicate rain and reduced visibility

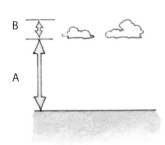

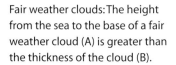

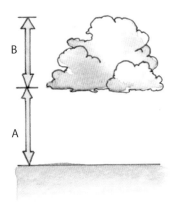

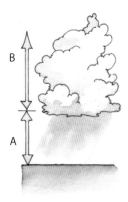

Fair weather clouds: The height from the sea to the base of a fair weather cloud (A) is greater than the thickness of the cloud (B).

Showers are possible when the height above the sea (A) becomes about equal to the thickness of the cloud (B). (A = B)

Showers accompanied by gusts are probable when the cloud (B) is thicker than the height of the cloud base above the sea (A). (B > A)

Making good use of high pressure. (Helen Tibbs)

Clouds are not just random events; any change in the clouds means something, although exactly what is not always apparent. Often, near land, cloud changes indicate thermal or mechanical activity in the atmosphere.

Lack of clouds signifies an area where the air is descending. It may be small-scale descent around cumulus clouds or large-scale descent found with high pressure. With any descent the air warms as it falls, hence any moisture tends to evaporate rather than condense.

Lapse Rate

The air cools with height at about 3.4°F/1,000ft (6.5°C/1,000m), depending on the moisture in the atmosphere. This is called the *lapse rate*. The atmosphere is rarely uniform though, so as we move upward through it there are bands of warmer and colder air. If we imagine a small parcel of air at the surface and heat it up a little, it will naturally rise but as it does it will also cool at approximately the lapse rate. It is the temperature of the air that surrounds our parcel that determines whether it continues to rise or stabilizes. It is therefore the temperature profile of the atmosphere that is important and the clouds are an indication of this profile.

CHAPTER 5

Lows

The majority of low-pressure systems (also known as depressions and sometimes marked as storms on weather maps) develop along the polar front. Over the oceans, the air circulates clockwise around the Pacific and Bermuda high-pressure systems. These are the semipermanent areas of high pressure found in the North Pacific and North Atlantic generated by global circulation, described in Chapter 2. This clockwise circulation of air moves heat and moisture north toward the polar front. In the Atlantic Ocean this is augmented by the Gulf Stream, which adds fuel in the form of heat. Along the front this warm, moist air meets cold, dry air arriving from the north, and the result is a breeding ground for lows. The illustrations on the following pages show this cycle in more detail. There is less moisture available over landmasses than over water, but the principle remains the same.

As the accompanying illustration shows, low-pressure systems have distinctive phases. Over time, because the cold front is moving faster than the warm front, it catches up, squeezing the warmer air in the warm sector off the surface as an *occluded front* is formed. Occluded fronts are a mixture of warm and cold front features and can be divided into warm and cold occlusions depending on the relative temperature of the air that is being caught up. When looking at a weather chart, if the occlusion is an extension of the cold front, then it is a cold occlusion, and if an extension of the warm front, a warm occlusion. Most occlusions tend to be cold occlusions and have many features of a cold front but are usually less violent. Warm occlusions have more warm front characteristics with heavy rain preceding them, quickly changing to post-cold-front conditions. In practical terms the difference between warm and cold occlusions is in the cloud structure and the amount of rain, which can be heavy.

On the weather chart, occluded fronts are shown as a mixture of the warm- and cold-front symbols and if drawn in color are purple.

Another feature of an occluded front is the way in which it can become bent back around the center of the low. Passing over and around the center, it produces a big band of cloud and rain.

As the low is generally filling in and slowing down, this band of heavy cloud can bring persistent rain that is reluctant to clear. Sailing under this band of cloud can be frustrating as the wind dies and often becomes variable in direction.

The Life Cycle of a Low

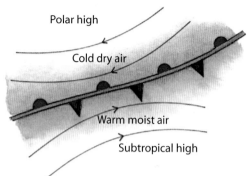

Stage 1. The polar front in equilibrium.

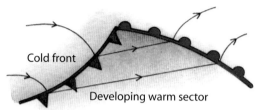

Stage 2. A disturbance in the upper atmosphere causes a wave to form on the polar front. The tongue of warm air in an area of generally cooler air causes a local reduction in pressure. This embryonic low pressure develops its own circulation, which helps make the wave even more pronounced.

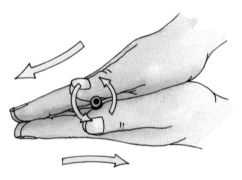

Hold a pencil between your hands and move in the direction of the arrows in the diagram. The pencil is like a disturbance on the polar front and will rotate like a fledgling depression.

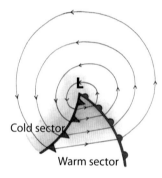

Stage 3. A full-blown low. The arrows show the wind direction for a low in the Northern Hemisphere. The surface wind is angled about 15° inward from the isobars toward the center of the low. Cold fronts and warm fronts are the leading edges of the air masses they describe. Thus the warm front in a low is the leading edge of the warm sector, with the warm air mass following on behind. The cold front is the leading edge of the cold sector.

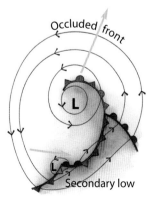

Stage 4. The low is in decline and shows a bent-back occlusion and a *secondary low* developing on the trailing cold front. This is not uncommon. Lows often form as families, each one tracking a little farther south until the thread is broken and a new polar front develops to the north.

As the low decays still further, the fronts will be seen to become detached from the low and the center expands to cover a greater area. This is the low going into decline, filling in and becoming a less significant feature on the weather charts.

Occlusions

Once occlusions begin to appear it is a sure sign that the low is reaching the end of its life cycle. Although the low may deepen for a further 6–12 hours after the fronts start occluding, it will then start decaying and filling in. As a general rule, the low will also start tracking farther to the left of where it had been heading—i.e., northward if the low is following its usual path from the west to east.

NON-FRONTAL LOWS

Although the majority of lows are created along the polar front, other forms of low pressure are also common throughout North America and the rest of the world; these can be grouped together under the heading of non-frontal lows.

The first of these are lee depressions and *lee troughing*, which are found downwind of mountains and high ground.

LEE DEPRESSIONS (LEE-SIDE LOWS)

As air flows over mountains and high land an area of low pressure develops in their lee (see illustration). It may develop as a trough or generate its own circulation and form a full-blown low. There are many well-known examples where this happens regularly. The eastern slope of the Rockies is such a place where lows form (or deepen). The mountains form

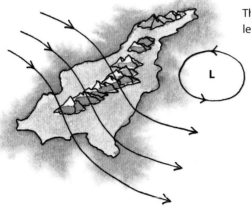

The flow of wind over a mountain range produces lee troughing and lee depressions.

a barrier to the wind and the lee-side low is a mechanical effect from the air being forced over the barrier. Initially the air is squeezed and changes direction in an anticyclonic (clockwise) direction, and then as it passes over the barrier it expands and lowers in pressure, curving in a cyclonic (counterclockwise) direction. This can happen anywhere that there are mountains across the flow of the wind. The mountains of New Zealand block the prevailing westerly wind; strong winds develop around their edges and a low forms in their lee. This will be discussed further in Chapter 10 on dangers; these strong winds may not show up on the sea-level pressure charts although they should be given in the local forecasts. One important thing to note about this is that sailing in the lee of mountains may not afford the shelter that you might expect.

HEAT, OR THERMAL, LOWS

During the summer months the heating of the land creates semipermanent low pressure areas. On a global scale, the bigger and hotter the landmass the more pronounced the low pressure. These heat lows affect the winds around them.

During the summer months an area of low pressure can usually be found on the weather charts over the desert in the southwest. With the semipermanent nature of the *Pacific High*, and the thermal low over the land, we get moderate to strong northwesterly winds along the Pacific coast. The wind will ease at night as the land cools and the pressure slowly rises, giving a daily regime of sea breeze followed by a calm night with a *land breeze* in places.

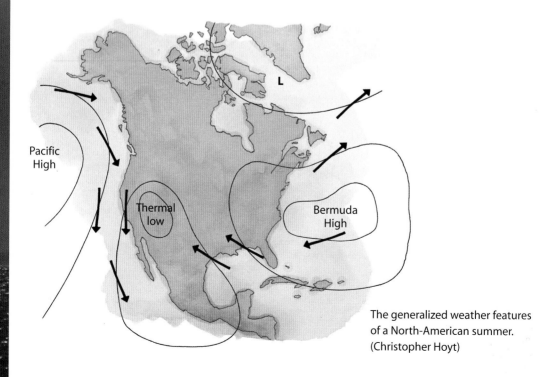

The generalized weather features of a North-American summer. (Christopher Hoyt)

Heat or thermal lows are found over all continents and have a significant effect on people's lives. Just two of many examples are the Indian Monsoon, which is largely driven by a heat low over India, and the Meltemi in the eastern Mediterranean, which is a consistent wind driven by the summer heat low over Turkey and Asia.

POLAR LOWS

The final form of depression is the polar low, caused when very cold Arctic air moves south during the winter, over a warmer sea. A small intense low can form bringing gale force winds and heavy snowfalls. The lows show up on satellite pictures as relatively small features, often with an *eye* in the center causing them to be referred to as Arctic hurricanes. They gain their energy from the temperature contrast between the relatively warm sea and the cold air. Once they move over land, their source of energy is switched off and they quickly decline.

Near our shores they can be found over the Labrador Sea and the Gulf of Alaska.

Buys Ballot's Law

The wind around a low spins counterclockwise in the Northern Hemisphere. This can be remembered by using Buys Ballot's Law, enunciated in 1857 by the Dutch meteorologist Christoph Buys Ballot. It states that when standing with your back to the wind, holding out your left arm will point to the center of low pressure. The opposite is true for the Southern Hemisphere.

Lows tend to dominate our weather. They are the features most likely to bring dangerous conditions, so they are also the ones we worry about the most. Thus it is no surprise that of the many old sailors' rhymes describing the weather, the majority warn of approaching lows and bad weather.

A Sailor's Rhyme

With a low and falling glass,
soundly sleeps a careless ass.
Only when 'tis high and rising,
soundly sleeps a careful wise one.

One of my favorite rhymes warning
of the danger as a low approaches.

COMPONENTS OF LOWS IN NORTH AMERICA

We have seen that lows will often develop well offshore, but they may deepen and form over the land. The tracks of most lows are through the northern parts of the U.S. from Washington state in the west to New England in the east, with the most frequent and strongest storms to the north. The southern states get fewer and weaker depressions. These are extra tropical cyclones and are distinct from the tropical storms and *hurricanes* that will be discussed later.

The tracks of lows are closely linked to the jet stream, a band of fast-moving air found around 6–9 miles (10–15km) above our heads. These "rivers" of wind travel in excess of 100 knots, sometimes as high as 200 knots, and although they meander north and south, the jet stream will usually move north in the summer and south during the winter. The position of the jet stream is often given in public weather forecasts on television.

The jet stream is found at a boundary between warm and cold air; this is also the boundary that is the polar front. Although the jet stream and surface conditions are not always in perfect alignment, the polar front and the jet stream are in close proximity.

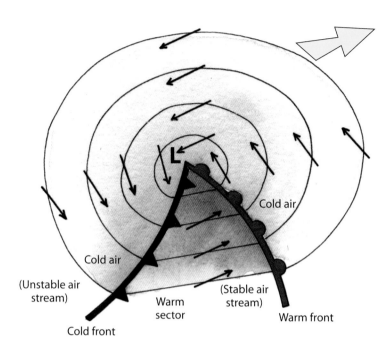

A typical Northern Hemisphere low. The black arrows show the surface wind and the yellow arrow the direction of the low's track.

Cold air

Cold air

(Unstable air stream)

(Stable air stream)

Warm sector

Warm front

Cold front

AHEAD OF THE WARM FRONT

Initially, we will look at what conditions are likely to be met if sailing south of the track of a low. This is not always the case, particularly if sailing in New England or more northerly latitudes, so we will look at what happens if the low is likely to come directly overhead, or pass south of us, at the end of this chapter.

Small cumulus clouds are fading as the upper-air cirrus clouds advance from the west. (Helen Tibbs)

The Anatomy of a Low

Cumulus clouds after the cold front has passed.

Stratus clouds in the warm sector.

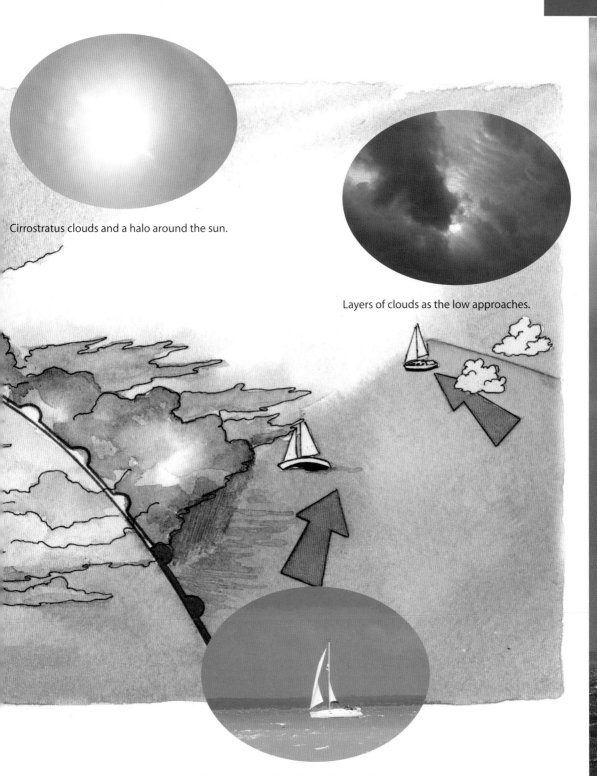

Cirrostratus clouds and a halo around the sun.

Layers of clouds as the low approaches.

Lowering clouds and rain ahead of the warm front. (Helen Tibbs photos)

A pleasant day's sailing with a few cumulus clouds around may be coming to an end as the cumulus clouds become fewer and high wispy clouds can be seen invading from the west. This sheet of cloud is usually the first indication that a low is on its way. The wispy clouds are made up of ice crystals and are known as cirrus. The speed at which the cirrus arrives indicates the speed of the low. "Hooks" (they look like fishhooks) in the clouds show that they are close to the jet stream, where winds in excess of 100 knots may be found at about 30,000ft.

As the cirrus invades, any cumulus clouds around are likely to decline in size and frequency, possibly making it hard to relate the current fine weather with a forecast of stronger winds and rain to follow. At this stage, the low pressure is typically still 600 miles away.

Early Indications of Low Pressure

■ High cirrus clouds (aka mares tails)

■ Wind backs to the south

■ Falling barometer

This gives rise to the old saying, "Backing winds and mares tails make tall ships carry low sails."

Backing—a change in the wind direction in a counterclockwise direction, e.g., from west to south.

Veering—the opposite of backing. A change in the wind direction in a clockwise rotation, e.g., from west to north. The terms hold true in either hemisphere.

The cirrus, however, is only the thin end of the wedge and provides the telltale sign of the warm front that divides the cool air from warm air following the front. This warm sector air is riding up and over the colder air along a slope of about 1 in 150. The front is still a long way away but as it advances, its height above our heads is reducing.

We have already seen that clouds form where there is a large-scale ascent of air (see Chapter 4 on clouds). The warm air rising up over the cold air gives us this large-scale ascent. As the warm air rises it cools, hence the clouds are formed.

As the low moves closer, the cirrus clouds thicken to form a whitish, milky veil or layer of clouds called cirrostratus. The sun appears hazy through this veil and often there is a *halo* around it. This halo is a luminous ring caused by the sunlight being refracted through ice crystals. Although it can occasionally be seen at other times it is usually an early indicator of the approaching warm front and low.

> The length of time between the cirrus arriving to losing the sun is usually about equal to the time from losing the sun to rain falling.

This halo phenomenon is not confined to the sun—it can also be seen around the moon, where it can be very clear and rather beautiful even though it may be an early indicator of deteriorating weather. A break in the halo is often said to indicate the direction the bad weather is coming from, although in practice it is usually caused by the low altitude of the sun or moon.

By now the wind should have backed to the south or southeast and the barometer will have started a slow steady fall. The speed with which the barometer falls indicates the depth of the low and how quickly it is moving, while how far the wind swings to the south indicates where the center of low pressure is likely to be. (Remember Buys Ballot's Law on page 25.) As the clouds thicken the halo disappears, and the sun looks as if it is shining through ground or frosted glass. This is altostratus—sheets of thickening lowering clouds giving a gloomy appearance that could best be described as blue-gray "mudflats" in the sky.

The approaching warm front lowers the clouds until it begins to rain. At first, the rain may appear to hang and not reach the surface, as scud (small ragged fragments of low clouds) rushes across the sky. Although the rain may start off fairly light, it will increase in intensity as the front approaches. A characteristic of the rain is that once it has started it is persistent, varying in intensity and becoming generally heavier as the layers of clouds thicken.

RAPIDLY FALLING BAROMETER

The faster a barometer falls, the stronger the wind we are likely to experience. As a rule of thumb, a 6mb drop in three hours indicates a Force 6 on the Beaufort scale (22–27 knots), while 8mb in three hours indicates a Force 8 (34–40 knots). Any faster sustained fall would indicate an even stronger blow.

A typical barometer next to the chart table. An occasional light tap is one way to ensure the needle is not stuck. (Chris Tibbs)

Approaching Warm Front

Clouds thicken and lower until it starts raining; rain can be heavy and persistent.

Barometer falls steadily. The faster the fall, the stronger the wind.

Wind backs to the south and increases.

Previously good visibility becomes poor in the rain.

Speed of the Front

Timing is always difficult in meteorology and becomes more so as the lows move over the land where the progress of the fronts may be interrupted.

The speed at which the warm front travels is a little slower than that of the surface wind speed behind it. This speed can be calculated more accurately from a weather chart, or a series of charts, if they are available (see Chapter 7). Listening to the forecast, however, will give an indication of where the front is, and its speed of movement can be estimated from the predicted wind behind the front.

Sitting in harbor waiting for the front to clear can be frustrating. The forecast wind may not be all that high, but few people enjoy sailing in the rain. Here the local land forecasts can help to plan the day as they are much more interested in the rain than wind.

The local land forecast will concentrate on where the rain is and when it is likely to clear. By correlating this with the sea area forecast and our knowledge of the behavior of the warm front, a good estimate can be made of when the wind will swing and when the rain will clear out.

Cold fronts travel at approximately the same speed as the surface wind behind them. As this is usually the strongest wind in a low, the cold front moves faster than the warm front, catching it up over time.

It is useful to remember that the low itself will usually follow a course that is parallel to the isobars in the warm sector.

AS THE WARM FRONT ARRIVES

A lightening of the sky to windward will herald the front, the heavy rain will ease, and a wind shift from south to southwest is to be expected. Shortly ahead of the front, the wind may actually back (i.e., swing a few degrees in a counterclockwise direction) a few degrees, although this is often missed unless you keep a very close weather eye. How much the wind veers (i.e., swings in a clockwise direction) on the front varies every time—it may only be small, or it may be 40 degrees or more.

AS THE WARM FRONT DEPARTS

The barometer should abruptly stop its downward plunge as the warm front passes and level off, becoming steady as we enter the warm sector. One of the less instantly recognizable changes is an increase in temperature—unless you are constantly monitoring with a thermometer, it is only after the rain has stopped that this becomes a recognizable feature.

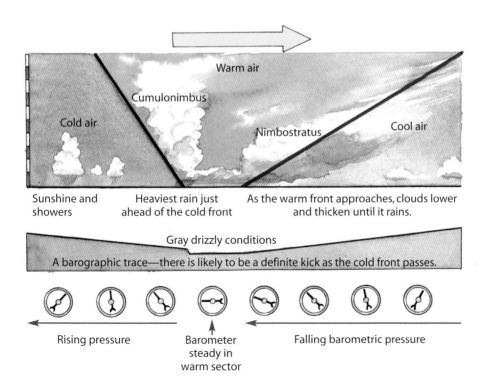

Warm air

Cumulonimbus

Cold air

Nimbostratus

Cool air

| Sunshine and showers | Heaviest rain just ahead of the cold front | As the warm front approaches, clouds lower and thicken until it rains. |

Gray drizzly conditions

A barographic trace—there is likely to be a definite kick as the cold front passes.

Rising pressure

Barometer steady in warm sector

Falling barometric pressure

As the Warm Front Arrives and Passes Through

- The sky will lighten on the windward horizon.
- There will be a break in the rain.
- The wind will veer from S to SW, but it may back a few degrees immediately ahead of the front.
- The barometer will fall more steadily.
- The air temperature will rise.
- Not all of these signs will be apparent on every warm front.

What to Expect in the Warm Sector

- A steady wind in direction and strength, usually from the SW.
- Steady pressure.
- Low cloud with some breaks.
- Warmer than before although it may be damp and drizzly.
- Moderate or poor visibility with fog possible.

Typical warm sector weather with low cloud and moderate or poor visibility. (Helen Tibbs)

WARM SECTOR WEATHER

The air in the warm sector is a tropical maritime air mass, meaning that it has spent its recent past life over warm seas and has acquired some of their characteristics (see air mass theory on page 5). The relative temperature and humidity of the air are high—hence the name "warm sector." This may give a muggy warm feeling and reduce the visibility in the warm sector.

As the air mass is cooled by the colder sea it is now passing over, it becomes increasingly stable; there will be less vertical movement in the air and the wind should be steady in both direction and strength. The barometer should also have leveled off. If the barometer is still falling, then the depression is still deepening or the center of the low is moving closer, and we can expect the wind to increase.

The clouds in the warm sector will bring drizzle or intermittent light rain and the visibility is usually poor with mist or fog likely. This depends mainly on the surface temperature of the sea; if it is cold compared to the air temperature, the lowest level of air will cool to below its dew point causing fog to appear. The speed of the wind will play its part as the stronger it blows the greater the mechanical turbulence and mixing, lifting the fog to a layer of low thick clouds. To still have fog around, the upper limit of the wind is usually 15 knots, the top end of Force 4.

The clouds in the warm sector vary enormously depending on the recent track of the low. On northwestern coasts, there is often rain and drizzle with poor visibility but on the East Coast, the air will have dried out while crossing the land. This can give quite different conditions between East and West Coast warm sectors. On the East Coast we often get active cold fronts sweeping off the land with no apparent warm front or sector present. On weather charts the cold front is shown and divides the different air masses.

The farther from the center of the low we are, the less cloud and rain we can expect. Although a low may be passing to the north, the farther south we are the more breaks in the cloud we are likely to see. The southern states may get a reasonable amount of sunshine during a warm sector, while close to the point where the warm and cold fronts meet, the cloud cover will be considerably thicker and the rain more persistent.

As the air mass is stable, convection is restricted and any breaks in the clouds will show that the upper clouds have all but gone.

On weather charts, the warm sector is recognizable by the almost parallel straight lines of the isobars between the warm and cold fronts. This gives a steady wind in both direction and strength; the actual strength depending on how close the isobars are together.

COLD FRONTS

The first sign of the approaching cold front is a thickening of the clouds. If there are any breaks in the clouds, then they will be seen reaching to much higher levels. As the clouds thicken and the rain starts, or intensifies, then the cold front is on its way. As it is not always possible to see the thicker clouds, the increase in rain is often the first sign of the cold front. There will not only be more of it, but the rain drops will be much larger. In fact, the whole characteristic of the rain changes.

Unstable air after a cold front. (Chris Tibbs)

Ahead of the cold front. (Helen Tibbs)

After a cold front passes clouds can form across the flow of the wind, producing a trough or mini front. (Helen Tibbs)

Stable air. (Helen Tibbs)

As the cold front arrives the rain intensifies and the wind becomes gustier. This is because it is coming from clouds that extend vertically up to 20,000 or 30,000 feet and produce large-sized raindrops. This band of heavy rain is usually around 50 miles wide although it can be double this, or it may be just a short shower.

Embedded in the clouds can be thunderclouds generating squalls and thunderstorms as the front goes through. The heavy rain can be taken as both a good and bad sign; bad because it can be quite unpleasant sailing in squally conditions and good because the cold front is nearly upon us and the weather will improve. A note of caution however; as the cold front passes, the wind is likely to increase in strength and swing quickly, sometimes violently, to the northwest becoming gusty and strong. Once the rain has stopped, visibility will greatly improve in the colder, clear air.

As the rain eases, a brighter band will be seen in the northwest. This band will move rapidly toward us as the front passes through.

Within a normal low one of the fronts is stronger than the other. It is usually the cold front that packs the punch, but this is not always the case. Looking at the weather charts, the isobars are usually the tightest behind the cold front, signifying where the strongest wind will be.

The wind behind the front will change. This is because the air mass has changed; the air is colder, usually coming from the northwest and probably not all that long ago it was over the Arctic, Canada, or even the North Pole.

Any dirt or pollution will have been washed out and the amount of moisture suspended in the air is low because of the colder nature of the air. This will therefore produce different cloud forms from those found in the warm sector. In fact, immediately behind the cold front there is often a band with no clouds at all. This will be followed by building cumulus and cumulonimbus clouds that, when big enough, will produce showers of building intensity, sometimes accompanied by hail or thunder. This is unstable air and will generate large convective clouds and showers. The instability will bring strong gusts.

As the Cold Front Passes

- The wind will back a few degrees then increase and veer. The change is likely to be in a squall and can be violent, sometimes with thunderstorms.
- Heavy rain ahead of the front will give way to a clearing sky.
- Pressure will start to rise, often with a kick.
- Visibility will be poor in the rain, but is becoming good.

WIND IN THE COLD FRONT

As the cold front approaches, the wind will increase a little and there is a good chance that it will back a few degrees. The often-torrential rain may disguise this to a certain extent, but as each front is different it may not back at all.

The wind will then become more blustery and veer to the northwest as the front goes through. Sometimes, but not often, we get a full 90-degree swing in the wind; most other times it will be much less. Weather maps and forecasts will help give an indication of how much the wind will swing and how strong it will get. After the front, the nature of the wind will have changed and we are now in a blustery, squally airstream. The wind behind the cold front is usually the strongest found in the low with the isobars packed closely together.

SUNSHINE AND SHOWERS

"Sunshine and showers" describes the weather behind the cold front. Some of these showers can be heavy: the large towering cumulus clouds following the front often fall into lanes and the showers they produce are not randomly scattered but follow down these lanes.

At other times, the clouds will form a band across the flow of the wind producing a trough or mini front—shown as a dashed line on weather charts. This trough will behave as a little cold front bringing a band of heavy rain, backing the wind a few degrees ahead of it, and veering on passing.

While this is going on, the barometer, which will have been steady or in slow decline during the warm sector, will give a sudden jump or "kick" as the front goes through. It will then start a steady and sometimes spectacular rise. A fast rise, like a fall, can bring strong winds leading to the saying "A quick rise after low predicts a stronger blow."

OCCLUDED FRONTS

In the section on the life cycle of a low we saw that over time lows will start to decline. The central pressure will be filling and the cold front will be catching the warm front, squeezing the warm sector and lifting the warmer air aloft. Where the fronts join they are said to occlude.

Where the fronts have occluded, the mixture of warm front and cold front clouds is likely to produce heavy rain, and a reluctance for the front to clear. Over land, the fronts can stall: such slow-moving occlusions and the prolonged heavy rain they produce are often the cause of flooding ashore.

The majority of occlusions are cold occlusions in which the air behind the cold front is colder than the air ahead of the warm front. As the cold air catches up it undercuts the warmer air. This means that the occlusion usually behaves more like a cold front than a warm front.

Canadian weather forecasts may refer to this is a TROWL: a trough of warm air aloft. This recognizes that the warm sector has been lifted from the surface and the sharp changes in weather associated with a cold front will not be as pronounced.

In practical terms, if we are waiting for a frontal system to pass through, an occlusion is likely to delay the arrival of the warm front, and more persistent rain is likely. We lose the drizzly conditions of the warm sector as the cold front combines with the warm.

The occluded front can become "bent back" around the center of the low, usually when the low is slow moving (see page 22). Where this happens the wind is likely to be light with big changes in direction, while the rain will be particularly heavy causing severely restricted visibility. The slow-moving front combined with the light wind and heavy rain does not make appealing sailing conditions.

Occluded front. (Helen Tibbs)

What to Expect with an Occluded Front

- Conditions ahead of an occluded front will be similar to those ahead of a warm front, with thickening and lowering clouds.
- The barometer will fall slowly.
- The rain will become heavier as the front arrives.
- The wind will slowly increase and may back a few degrees ahead of the occlusion before veering on the passage of the front and becoming blustery.
- As the front passes through, the rain will clear and the clouds give way to sunshine and showers.
- The barometer will start to rise.

WHEN A LOW PASSES TO THE SOUTH

If we are north of the low's track we will miss the changes in weather associated with the passing of the fronts. How far to the south the low passes will determine how cloudy and rainy it will be; the farther away from the center, the less cloudy and rainy. The wind, however, can be strong and will gradually back as the low passes. This can cause some problems if the low is tracking farther south than usual, as normally sheltered anchorages may become exposed in easterly winds. The wind will continue to gradually back, as the low passes to the south. How quickly it backs will depend on the size of the low, the speed at which it is traveling, and our distance from it. Some of the worst conditions found on the New England coast are from a *"Nor'easter,"* which can be particularly bad in the winter. They are created from a deep low (cyclonic storm) passing to the south giving gale or storm force onshore winds.

WHEN A LOW PASSES OVERHEAD

If you are on track for the low to pass overhead, conditions can get quite difficult. There will be thick layers of clouds and heavy rain; the wind will remain fixed in the southerly sector as the low approaches. The barometer will continue to fall until the wind lightens and becomes almost calm; this is when the center is overhead. When the wind returns, it is from the opposite direction and will most likely build quickly. The barometer will indicate when the center has passed through with a quick rise. One of the worst aspects of a low passing close overhead is a confused and uncomfortable sea as the wind changes direction. In a forecast, the wind may well be described as "cyclonic."

It is unusual to have the low pass directly overhead although it has happened to me a few times. The most dramatic occasion was when racing in the Southern Ocean; the wind went from 50 knots to nothing, then back to 50 knots from the opposite direction, all in the space of a four-hour watch. The sea could only be described as chaotic and rather dangerous!

The First Sign of a New Low

On weather maps, the first sign of a new low being born is when the cold front runs parallel to the isobars. The whole system slows down and along the front the symbols change from those of a cold front to those of a warm front. The isobars separate, and on successive charts closed circulation is seen.

Between each low we often get a ridge of high pressure with light winds and some clearing of the sky. However, this can be short-lived as the next low quickly arrives. As a rule—if, after a cold front, the showers you expect do not materialize, another low could be on its way.

FAMILIES OF LOWS

A low that has developed along the polar front is unlikely to arrive on its own: it is more likely to be one of a family of lows. This is the unsettled weather of the winter months that all too often edges its way into the summer as one low follows another.

As the low occludes and declines, the cold front can often be seen to extend all the way to the southwest from the center of the low. This will be over the Pacific if we have a low approaching from the West Coast; however it may extend across North America if the parent low is out in the Atlantic. The conditions in the slow-moving part of the front are very similar to the conditions that caused the first low to form, so a disturbance along this front will cause another low to be born. This is the start of a family of lows, each one starting life on the old cold front of the previous low.

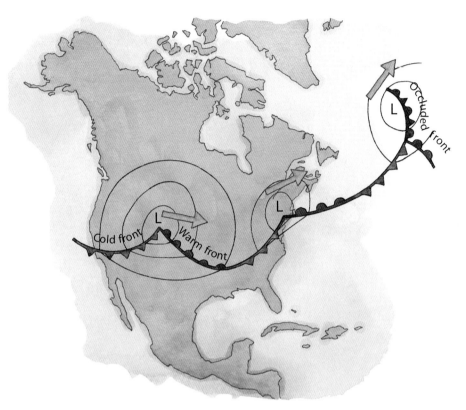

Families of lows can dominate weather patterns, as shown here over North America.
(Christopher Hoyt)

There are no hard and fast rules but a typical family is made up of four or five lows. Each one develops successively to the southwest and follows a track to the south of the original path of the low. Eventually the sequence is broken and the next low develops way to the north and a new generation is started.

SECONDARY LOWS

A secondary low is a depression embedded in the flow around the main or primary low. As the primary low weakens, the secondary low can quickly deepen and become the dominant feature, swallowing up the original low or "dumbbelling" around it.

A secondary low may develop at any of several places, but the most common is after the low has occluded, at the *triple point* where the cold front, warm front, and occlusion meet.

Although this is not uncommon, by no means do all triple points create a secondary low. If one does occur we can see a rapid and dramatic fall in pressure over a short time, often to below that of the primary low.

On a weather chart, the first sign of a secondary low forming is the widening of the isobars before an area of closed circulation forms around the triple point.

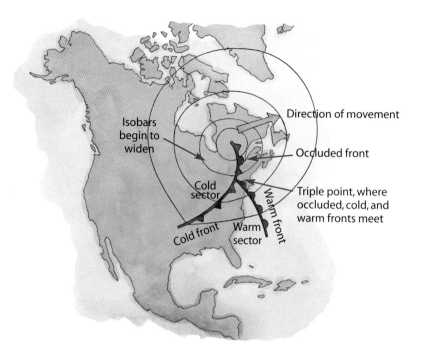

Development of a secondary low.
(Christopher Hoyt)

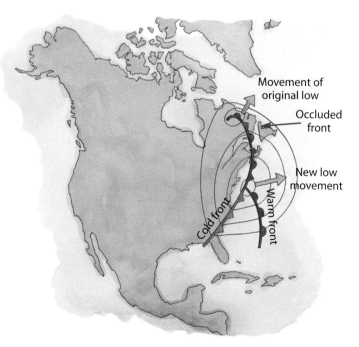

A secondary low developing at the triple point. (Christopher Hoyt)

Although the area between the secondary low and its parent usually has widely spaced isobars and correspondingly light winds, the side of the secondary that is farthest from the parent often has much stronger winds. What makes secondary lows dangerous is that they—and their associated strong winds—often develop in as little as 12–24 hours, and only after the occlusion and weakening of the parent low has lulled the unwary into a false sense of security.

> ## Secondary Low
>
> On a weather chart the first sign of a secondary low forming is the widening of the isobars before an area of closed circulation forms around the triple point.
>
> As a rule of thumb, the secondary low has to be greater than 600 miles away from the parent low for it to really deepen and become the dominant feature.

TROUGHS

A trough of low pressure is something that we often see on our weather charts. It is marked by a dashed line in the U.S., often a solid line on charts from other sources, and may well have the word "Trough" or "Trof" written beside it (see art next page).

The trough may be caused by heating of the land and is named a thermal or heat trough. These are semipermanent in nature; a good example of this is the thermal low or trough that develops in the southwest United States over the deserts. (See Chapter 13.)

Most troughs on the surface weather charts are, however, linked with transient lows moving from the west to east. The isobars will curve away from the low-pressure center like a small front. Thinking of a trough in terms of a small cold front is useful as there are many similarities. While all fronts are marked by a trough, the converse is not true. However, troughs will usually produce showery unsettled weather with instability in the atmosphere giving gusts and squalls. There may be a veer in the wind after the trough has passed.

Sometimes when sailing in the northwest flow after a cold front has passed through, we get a trough or series of troughs. They are visible as bands of clouds approaching often with showers. Rather than the occasional shower expected with the unstable northwest flow, these appear as an organized band of clouds or squall lines. The wind will pick up, often by 10 knots or so. A sharp shower follows and there will often be a veer in the wind direction, which is sometimes temporary but usually permanent. How active the trough is will vary, but if the clouds look dark and stormy the trough will be active and the gusts will be strong.

We also sometimes see a trough line drawn between two low-pressure centers within a family of lows. This will be typified by the rain and instability of the above feature but may be slow moving.

A trough that can have serious weather with it is a pre-frontal trough or pre-frontal squall line. This is a trough ahead of a fast-moving cold front and moving parallel with it. It is typified by severe thunderstorms and squalls with their associated *gust fronts*. These may be of gale force or stronger. At times the squalls and thunderstorms can be 200 miles ahead of the front, in the axis of the pre-frontal trough.

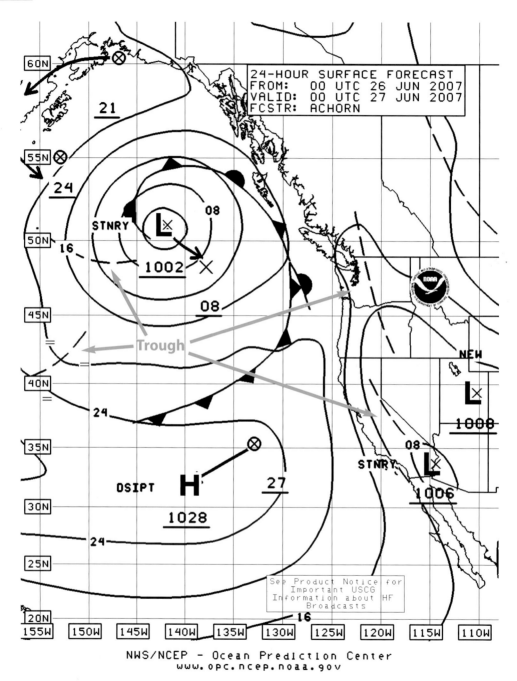

A weather chart for the eastern Pacific with troughs marked by dashed lines. (National Weather Service)

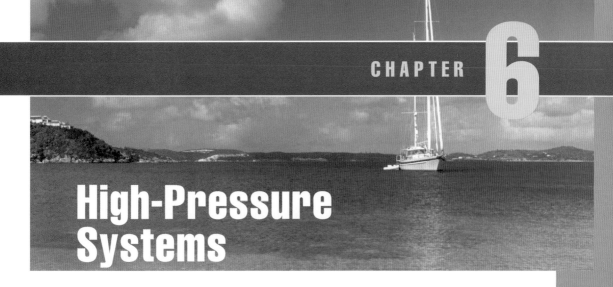

CHAPTER 6

High-Pressure Systems

The opposite of low pressure is high pressure. That may sound like stating the obvious, but it's important to appreciate that in meteorology, the words "high" and "low" are relative to the surrounding pressures, and that it is impossible to say that a pressure over Xmb is "high" or that one below Ymb is "low."

As one might expect from the idea of a high being the opposite of a low, the circulation of air around a high is clockwise in the Northern Hemisphere (and counterclockwise in the Southern Hemisphere). This is the opposite of the cyclonic circulation found around a low,

High pressure over the ocean, here characterized by light wind and few clouds.
(Bluegreen Pictures)

and gives us the term *anticyclone* as an alternative, more technical-sounding word for "high."

Also, whereas lows are characterized by surface air flowing upward and inward generating clouds, the airflow in a high is downward and outward, usually resulting in clear skies.

TYPES OF HIGHS

SEMIPERMANENT HIGHS

The global circulation (see Chapter 2) should, in theory, produce a band of high pressure in each hemisphere, about 30–40 degrees north and south of the equator. In reality, the presence of continental landmasses breaks up these bands, leaving several distinct semipermanent areas of high pressure. In the North Atlantic, for instance, there is the Bermuda High, while its counterpart in the south is called the South Atlantic or Saint Helena High. In the Pacific we have the Pacific High sitting off the West Coast and a corresponding South Pacific High in the Southern Hemisphere.

These areas of high pressure move with the seasons, drifting south in the northern winter and north in the summer. Their centers will also move east and west as they decline and intensify; however they are usually there in one shape or another. They are a little like partially filled water balloons that can be squeezed and pushed around, changing shape as other weather systems move by.

Most lows stay north of these highs, their tracks being guided by the high's position. Stationary high pressure may get referred to as a *blocking high* diverting lows away, bringing long periods of settled weather.

The position, pressure, and extent of the Pacific High has an important effect on the track of lows crossing the Pacific and whether they will hit the Pacific Northwest coast or be diverted toward Alaska. The size and intensity of the Bermuda High has a significant effect on East Coast weather, as well as shaping the track of Atlantic storms.

TRANSIENT HIGHS

Transient highs or ridges appear between the low-pressure areas within a family of lows (see illustration). Although smaller and shorter-lived than semipermanent highs, transient highs have similar characteristics, and provide a respite from the wet and windy weather associated with the lows.

Showers and squalls associated with the passing cold front will decrease as clouds become fewer and farther apart. The wind will ease in strength as the high pressure moves overhead. How long this will last depends on the speed of the next low approaching from the west. The first sign will be the approach of upper level clouds and a swing in the wind (typically) to the southeast. The clouds will lower and the barometer will fall as the low approaches. See Chapter 5 for a full description on weather conditions expected ahead of a low.

Racing in the Southern Ocean, as one depression followed another, we were given the occasional respite as the skys cleared and the wind dropped. This was the ridge of high pressure between the lows. It lasted from a few hours to half a day before the wind picked

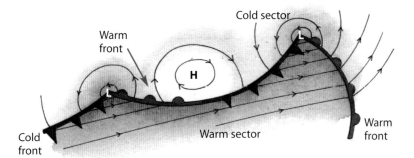

A transient anticyclone (high) between two low-pressure systems.

up again and rain returned—long enough to open hatches and get some fresh air, but not long enough to dry out!

SAILING IN HIGH PRESSURE

Offshore, the wind in a high-pressure area is likely to be steady. Its strength is related to the spacing between isobars, but as high-pressure areas generally have widely spaced isobars, the wind is most likely to be light, particularly near the center. Toward the edges, though, particularly in the *squeeze zone* between a high and low pressure (see page 87), the isobars may be tightly packed, with a strong pressure gradient producing strong winds.

Nearer the coast, a high is most likely to produce light winds, falling calm overnight and with the possibility of coastal fog in the early hours of the morning. Small cumulus clouds or sheets of stratocumulus may form, but the usual picture—particularly in summer—is for cloud-free days and nights, sometimes with poor visibility caused by dust or pollution trapped in the lowest level of the atmosphere.

The Transpac race from Los Angeles to Hawaii has become a classic downwind race skirting the Pacific High pressure system. Seldom does the rhumb line route (the straight line course) prove to be the fastest as this passes close to the center of the high and into light winds. A longer route keeping in good breeze without adding too many miles is generally the faster course; however getting this "just right" is the difference between winning and losing.

Over land, high pressure in winter is responsible for our coldest temperatures, and may give rise to a phenomenon known as an *inversion* in which temperature increases with height instead of decreasing. This traps fog, clouds, or polluted air close to the surface, producing poor visibility, *and* smog. This is sometimes called *anticyclonic gloom*.

Sailing with high-pressure conditions during the winter months. (Bluegreen Pictures)

Pollution trapped under an inversion during high pressure. (Chris Tibbs)

CHAPTER 7

Predicting the Wind from Weather Charts

There is a definite relationship between expected wind and the spacing of isobars on a weather chart. Therefore, by measuring the isobar spacing and making a few adjustments, it is possible to make a good estimate of the expected wind strength.

One of the best means to predict wind speed is by analyzing weather charts. Weather charts, or synoptic charts, are generally issued in series. Each series starts with an "analysis chart," showing the actual situation as it was recorded at various weather stations at a particular time—usually 00 or 12 hours UTC (see sidebar on page 52). The series continues with charts showing the expected situation at regular intervals—usually either 12 or 24 hours—over the next five or six days. (See Weather Briefing Packages on page 141.)

Some sources publish analysis charts at different times, some produce forecast charts at longer or shorter intervals, and some cover longer or shorter periods. They all allow us to see how fronts and pressure systems are expected to move, and thereby predict what the weather is likely to be. It's important to appreciate, though, that the production of forecast charts is still not an exact science, so their accuracy almost inevitably is reduced the farther ahead they forecast for. Here are some tips to read charts to help predict wind.

- Comparing the central pressures of weather systems on successive charts shows whether they are rising or falling.
- A low generally moves parallel to the isobars in its warm sectors, but turns toward the pole once its fronts start to occlude.
- Cold fronts move at about the speed of the *geostrophic wind* (see page 52) measured at the front.
- Warm fronts move at about 2/3rds of the speed of the geostrophic wind.

There is a direct relationship between pressure gradient, as shown on the weather charts by the isobars and how far apart they are, and wind speed; by measuring the distance between the isobars we can get an approximation of the theoretical wind speed. This gives

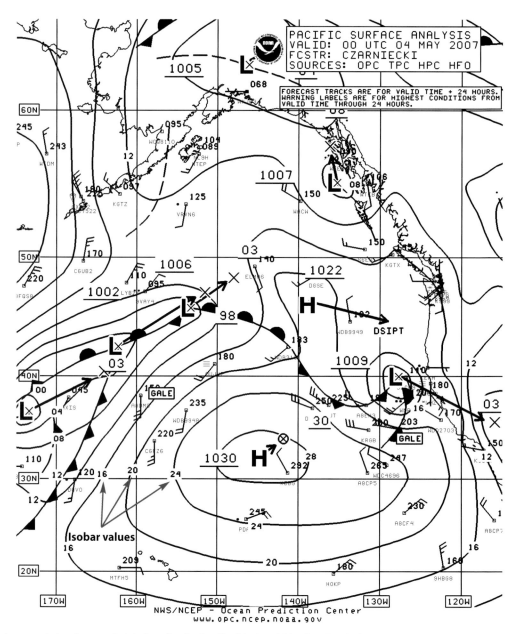

A synoptic (surface analysis) chart for the Pacific. (National Weather Service)

the wind that would be blowing if all the isobars were straight and parallel, and represents the balance between the pressure gradient and the effect of the spinning earth (Coriolis force). This is called the geostrophic wind.

There are a number of ways to do this; computers use long mathematical formulae and some charts, mainly in Europe, have a wind scale on them. However the majority of the charts that you will come across will not, so some way of measuring the distance between the isobars and converting this to wind speed from a table is necessary. Measure the distance between two isobars with dividers (see photos): use a place where the isobars are straight and parallel, and measure at right angles to the isobars.

This distance must now be translated into nautical miles (nm). The most straightforward way is to compare the measured distance with latitude as all charts have latitudes marked. (Remember that one degree of latitude is 60 miles; therefore 5 degrees is 300 miles.) Measure the distance at the latitude near where the isobars were measured to keep the estimated distance as accurate as possible.

Weather charts usually show latitude marked in 10° spacing, sometimes in 5°. In our example the spacing is in 10° segments as seen on the labels on the left-hand side of the chart. We measured the isobar spacing near 40°; therefore we need to calculate the distance near 40°. I have split the 10° into 4, to give me an easier scale to work with. We can see from the picture that when measured against the latitude scale the isobar spacing is 2.5°, which equates to 150nm (2.5 × 60nm).

Once we have the isobar spacing then we can enter this into the accompanying geostrophic wind speed table. This gives us a geostrophic wind speed of 24 knots. It can be seen from the table that choosing the wrong latitude makes a big difference; at 20° the same spacing would give a wind speed of 45 knots and at 60° just 18 knots.

If the weather map is displayed on a computer screen, a piece of acetate with a scale marked is a good substitute for the dividers (and is a lot kinder to the screen).

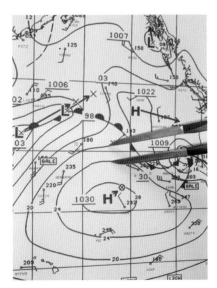

Using dividers to measure space between isobars. (Helen Tibbs)

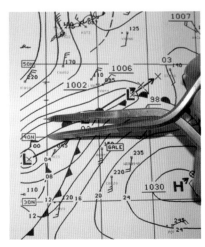

Moving the measured distance between isobars to the synoptic chart's latitude scale. (Helen Tibbs)

Geostrophic Wind Speed Table

Latitude	Distance (nm) between 4mb Isobars						
	50	60	80	100	150	200	300
	Geostrophic Wind Speed in Knots						
20°	136	113	85	68	45	34	23
30°	92	77	57	46	31	23	15
40°	72	60	45	36	24	18	12
50°	60	50	38	30	21	15	10
60°	53	44	33	26	18	13	9

Having measured the geostrophic wind speed, we have to modify it to get the *gradient wind*. The difference between the two is the result of the air curving around weather systems. Around low pressure the air slows. The tighter the curve, the more the wind slows. Conversely, around high pressure the wind speed increases—the tighter the curve the greater the increase.

As the amount that the wind slows or increases depends on the tightness of the curvature, no adjustment is necessary if we can find a place where the isobars are straight. Very tight curvature will decrease the wind around a low or increase it around a high by 25 percent. In extreme cases, the gradient wind around a high can be double the geostrophic wind.

Geostrophic → Gradient → Surface

As a rule of thumb, but not as accurate as working it through:

Over the sea, the surface wind speed is about 2/3rds of the geostrophic wind speed in low-pressure systems and backed by about 15 degrees.

Over the land, the surface wind speed is about half the geostrophic wind.

Coordinated Universal Time (UTC)

UTC is Coordinated Universal Time and is the local time based on Greenwich, near London, England. This is where the Greenwich meridian or 0° longitude is situated and is used as a worldwide standard. The time zone on the East Coast of the United States is UTC-5 and the Pacific UTC-8; these need further adjustment for daylight saving. Throughout the meteorology world, the 24-hour clock is used.

UTC replaces the older term GMT (Greenwich Mean Time), which may also be referred to as "Zulu" in marine circles.

As no system is ever nicely round in shape, it is difficult to get a very accurate result. It pays to be on the conservative side and adjust your result to account for the worst the wind is likely to throw at you. This is safer than overcorrecting and getting a stronger wind than expected. As a rule, unless the isobars are very tightly curved, restrict any adjustment to 10 percent for low pressure, 20 percent for high.

With this adjustment, we now have the gradient wind—the wind found above the boundary layer at around 2000 feet (600 meters), a height unaffected by the surface.

We now have to modify this forecast to allow for the effects of surface friction. This will vary depending on the stability of the atmosphere; here you will need to make a judgment on the air mass where you have taken the measurement as well as on the surface concerned.

The accompanying table shows the multiplier to be used to convert the gradient wind speed to the surface wind speed, and the amount by which the direction of the surface wind should be shifted.

We now have an expected surface wind, in knots, for the time marked on the weather map. From our previous example, we measured the geostrophic wind as 24 knots. This was in a place where the isobars were straight and parallel so we do not need to make an adjustment for curvature. As we measured the wind speed on the edge of the high pressure, the air mass is stable. The surface wind speed over the sea in these stable conditions is therefore 18 knots (24 knots × .75 = 18 knots).

We have almost finished but not quite. On an average day, we can expect gusts of up to a third again as high as the given wind speed. These gusts can be stronger in unstable conditions around big showers and squalls, and less with stable conditions. The expected wind speed in our example would be 18 knots with gusts up to 24 knots.

It is unlikely that our position is exactly in between isobars, and even if it is, the systems will move. We must look at the expected winds around the area, how the gradient changes, and whether we will find stronger or lighter winds as we proceed.

Weather maps cover a large area; it is a good idea to verify the analysis as best you can. On board, this is done by checking that the barometer is accurately adjusted and by noting the wind direction and strength. Observations of cloud structures will indicate where within a system you might be, and the likely air mass.

If Internet access is available, you will be able to find barometer readings and weather reports from some coastal stations and airports, buoy reports, and satellite images. (Chapter 12 looks at this in more detail.)

Surface Wind Calculator

Conditions	Over Sea		Over Land	
	Speed multiplier	Degrees backed	Speed multiplier	Degrees backed
Cold clear night			0.25	40
Stable	0.75	20	0.33	35
Unstable	0.90	10	0.60	20
Average	0.80	15	0.50	30

Stable means, for example, the warm sector of a low- or a high-pressure area. Unstable means, for example, the cold sectors of a low.

Measuring the Wind Speed from the Weather Map

1. Using dividers, measure the distance between isobars.

2. Still using the dividers, estimate the distance in miles (nm) between the isobars. The latitude is useful for this; one degree equals 60nm.

3. Using the distance in nm, enter distance and latitude into the geostrophic wind speed table and read the geostrophic wind speed.

4. Were the isobars straight and parallel where measured?

5. If not, adjust for curvature (– for lows, + for highs).

6. We now have gradient wind.

7. Adjust for surface friction (using the table).

8. Make allowances for gusts.

Verifying the forecast. Do conditions match those expected?

ADDITIONAL METHODS FOR MEASURING WIND SPEED FROM WEATHER CHARTS

Similar to our previous method, but also useful on charts that have nonstandard 4mb isobar spacing, we can measure the number of isobars over a 300nm distance and use a multiplier from the accompanying table. The distance of 300nm is convenient as it is 5 degrees of latitude, and all charts have latitude marked at either 5- or 10 degree spacing.

By setting the dividers to 300nm, we measure the pressure change over this distance. Let us assume for our example that there is a 10mb pressure change over the 300nm covering the area that we are sailing.

If this is at 55 degrees (e.g., southern Alaska), by using the multiplier from the table we multiply the 10mb by 2.4 giving a geostrophic wind speed of 24 knots.

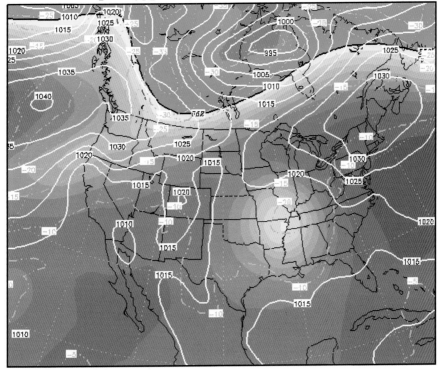

Each isobar is marked with its value although the first one or two digits may be removed for clarity (e.g., an isobar marked 20 is 1020mb). (Wetterzentrale.de)

Geostrophic Wind Speed Calculator

Latitude (degrees)	Multiplier
60	2.3
55	2.4
50	2.6
45	2.8
40	3.1
35	3.4
30	3.9

Likely wind speed units found in weather forecasts:
1 knot = 1 nautical mile per hour = 1.15 mph = 0.51 meters per second

Wind Direction Nomenclature

The wind direction given in forecasts refers to where the wind is coming from, i.e., a northerly wind is a wind blowing from the north. Only the main eight points of the compass are generally used; dividing the wind direction much more implies an accuracy that is unlikely to be met. Actual reports of wind conditions are sometimes given in degrees (true) or using a 16-point compass, making it a useful exercise to look at the chart and use the compass rose on it to see the direction.

The Beaufort Scale

The *Beaufort scale* was developed by Admiral Francis Beaufort in an effort to standardize weather reports. The scale was first published in 1808, long before *anemometers* were available. Beaufort's scale linked wind strength to the sea state and the amount of sail that could be carried by the British naval ships of the time. Nowadays, the Beaufort scale still links wind speed with the sea state that can be expected in open waters away from the influence of land or tidal flow. It can also be adapted to the amount of sail a cruising yacht may be expected to carry.

   This easily understood scale is still widely used around the world as a way of expressing wind strength in marine weather forecasts and reports. However, in the U.S. and Canada the main form of expressing wind in marine forecasts is in knots, and if there is a description (e.g., gales), this refers to the Beaufort scale. For land forecasts this will usually be in mph (km/hr in Canada).

continued

The Beaufort Scale Illustrated

Force 1
Light air: 1–3 knots.
Ripples.
Sail—drifting conditions.
Power—fast planing conditions.

Force 2
Light breeze: 4–6 knots.
Small wavelets.
Sail—full mainsail and large genoa.
Power—fast planing conditions.

Force 3
Gentle breeze: 7–10 knots.
Occasional crests.
Sail—full sail.
Power—fast planing conditions.

Force 4
Moderate: 11–16 knots.
Frequent white horses.
Sail—reduce headsail size.
Power—may have to slow down if wind against tide.

Force 5
Fresh breeze: 17–21 knots.
Moderate waves, many white crests.
Sail—reef mainsail.
Power—reduce speed to prevent slamming when going upwind.

Force 6
Strong breeze: 22–27 knots.
Large waves, white foam crests.
Sail—reef main and reduce headsail.
Power—displacement speed.

Force 7
Near gale: 28–33 knots.
Sea heaps up, spray, breaking waves, foam blows in streaks.
Sail—deep reefed main, small jib.
Power—displacement speed.

Force 8
Gale: 34–40 knots.
Moderately high waves, breaking crests.
Sail—deep reefed main, storm jib.
Power—displacement speed, stem waves (i.e., you may have to slowly motor into the waves).

Force 9
Severe gale: 41–47 knots.
High waves, spray affects visibility.
Sail—trysail and storm jib.
Power—displacement speed, stem waves.

Force 10
Storm: 48–55 knots.
Very high waves, long breaking crests.
Survival conditions.

Force 11
Violent storm: 56–63 knots.
Exceptionally high seas with continuously breaking waves seriously affecting visibility.
Survival tactics.

Force 12
Hurricane: 64 knots and above.
Exceptionally high seas with continuously breaking waves seriously affecting visibility.
Survival tactics.

CHAPTER 8

Land's Effect on the Wind

Having listened to the forecast, downloaded synoptic charts from the Internet, or received them by fax, it is now time to add our own input into the picture that makes up the weather puzzle.

Almost by definition, our starting and finishing points are sheltered. The passage between them often follows the coast, so unless we are well away from the land, we must always consider how the proximity of land is likely to change the wind. Just how far away from the land we need to be for the wind and weather to be unaffected is a little like asking "how long is a piece of string?"

Ten or twelve miles is a rule of thumb, but it varies depending on whether the wind is blowing offshore, onshore, or parallel to the coast. A good sea breeze in the spring or early summer may extend even farther. Mountains and high land in the stream of wind may influence the wind for many miles, as anyone caught in the wind shadow of one of the larger Caribbean islands will know. However not all mountains cause a wind shadow—the *Santa Ana wind* of Southern California rushes down the mountain canyons from the elevated desert plateau. This can bring strong to gale force winds to coastal waters with little warning. In rivers and landlocked venues we need to look at the land forecast and modify it for over the water, while near the coast we can use the sea forecast and modify it for the influence of the land.

Air, like water, looks for a path of least resistance. The greater the number of rocks and obstructions in a stream, the greater the disturbance to the general flow. The wind is like this on a much larger scale. Thinking of it in these terms can help understand why the wind behaves as it does around land.

How the land modifies the wind can be split conveniently into two processes—mechanical and thermal effects.

Naming the Wind

In marine weather forecasting we use the direction the wind is coming *from* to name the wind. So, for instance, a "northerly" is a breeze blowing from the north. The following terms are used around the world.

Onshore—the wind is blowing *onto* the coast.

Offshore—the wind is blowing *away* from the coast.

Alongshore—the wind is blowing *parallel* to the coast.

MECHANICAL EFFECTS

We have already discussed the fact that the wind has a direct relationship with the pressure gradient—represented on weather maps by spacing between the isobars. This, however, is the gradient wind at about 2000 feet (600m) where it is undisturbed by the surface. In Chapter 7, we looked at ways of estimating the gradient wind from weather maps.

The *Coriolis force* tends to make the wind at higher levels (above about 600m) blow parallel to the isobars. At ground or sea level, however, the moving air is slowed down by friction, and the Coriolis force is reduced so the wind is diverted more toward the center of low pressure.

How much the wind is slowed and deflected depends on the roughness of the surface and on the buoyancy of the air. Over land, there is a big difference between smooth grassy fields and the rough surface of forests or cities. Forests or cities reduce the wind speed more than open fields, and increase the extent to which it is backed (however, around high buildings there are strong gusts and eddies even when the general wind is light). By comparison, even a "rough" sea is effectively smooth, so the wind is slowed down and diverted to a much lesser extent.

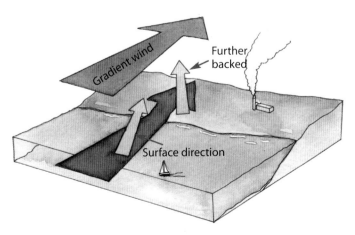

The effect of drag on wind direction over the land and the sea.

As a rule of thumb, the surface wind over the sea will be about 80–90 percent of the gradient wind, and will be angled inward from the isobars by about 10–15 degrees (see Chapter 7). Over land, it will be about 50 percent of the gradient wind, and will be angled inward by about 30 degrees. The change of wind speed and direction is not instantaneous: an offshore wind doesn't immediately change direction and increase in speed as it crosses the coast.

> As a rule of thumb, in average conditions the surface wind over the sea will be about 80–90 percent of the gradient wind, while over land it will be closer to 50 percent of the gradient wind.

The difference between the surface wind and the gradient wind can often be seen from the movement of low clouds. If you stand facing the surface wind, the clouds (in the Northern Hemisphere) will usually be seen approaching from your right, because they are being blown along by the gradient wind.

STABILITY AND INSTABILITY

Stability and instability refer to the relationship between the air near the surface and the air above it. Temperature is a particularly important factor in this relationship.

Remember that air is not affected by heat from the sun shining through it, but is changed by the temperature of the surface below. This therefore heats or cools the air from the lowest levels upward, thus changing the buoyancy of the air, causing it either to rise or sink.

If the air is being heated from below, it will rise—along with the water held in it—giving a buoyant or unstable atmosphere. If, however, the air at surface level is being cooled it will stay where it is and be stable.

Stable Versus Unstable Conditions

Stable Conditions	Unstable Conditions
Steady surface wind	Gusty conditions
Layer clouds—stratus or no clouds at all	Cumulus clouds; any rain will be showers
Poor visibility and possible fog	Good visibility outside of showers
Occurs typically in warm sector or high pressure	Occurs typically after a cold front or thunderstorms

THERMAL EFFECTS

Over land the surface temperature has a strong daily cycle as the land heats during the day and cools at night. Over the sea, however, there is little change in the temperature throughout a 24-hour period. In the absence of a change of air mass from a synoptic scale system,

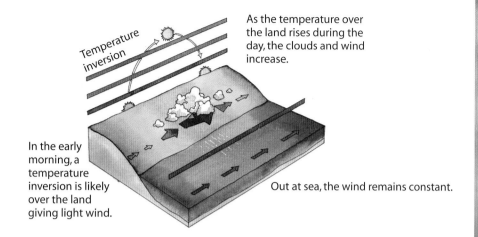

Temperature inversion

As the temperature over the land rises during the day, the clouds and wind increase.

In the early morning, a temperature inversion is likely over the land giving light wind.

Out at sea, the wind remains constant.

or strong winds, the temperature and wind changes throughout the day are shown in the accompanying illustration.

Fast-moving deep lows and large-scale synoptic conditions will override local thermal effects but, on the majority of summer days, there will be some thermal influence. We have all seen days when it is flat calm early in the morning, but by mid-afternoon we are reefed down, only for the wind to drop again at night. This is the typical wind pattern throughout the day near coasts, particularly in the summer, when there are no large weather systems around bringing clouds, strong winds, or changes in air mass.

Over the land, the temperature rises to a peak in the early afternoon and falls to a minimum around dawn.

This diurnal change in temperature means that the land is warmer than the air during the day but colder at night. This has the effect of changing the stability of the air from unstable during the day, to stable at night.

During the night, as the land cools, it in turn cools the bottom layers of the atmosphere, making it become more stable. We have already seen that the more stable the air is, the greater the effect of drag on the wind. This is the start of a feedback mechanism: the land cools the air, the air becomes more stable and is slowed by friction, so the cooling earth has a greater effect on the air, cooling and slowing it still further. This can stop the wind completely, often giving calm conditions over land on clear cold nights. Gravity helps drain this cold air down rivers and out over coastal waters creating a band of light wind around the coasts.

This continues until dawn, which is the coldest part of the night. It also creates an inversion in the temperature at the bottom of the atmosphere, with the air getting warmer with height rather than colder. Above the inversion and the boundary layer, the gradient wind is still blowing—indeed there may be a stronger band created above the boundary layer (known as a *nocturnal jet*).

Obviously the clearer and colder the night, the greater the chance of the wind dropping. The effect spreads to coastal waters giving quiet nights at anchor when cruising in the summer.

Calm conditions are often found at night. (Helen Tibbs)

Once the sun gets to work heating the land, the inversion begins to break down. It does, however, need the vertical movement of the warming air to break the inversion and get the flow of air mixing again before we will feel any surface wind. A sign of the inversion breaking down is the development of cumulus clouds over the land.

As the day progresses and the ground warms, the boundary layer begins to heat. This reduces the stability giving more vertical movement to the air. This mixing increases the surface wind as the land heats and some of the gradient wind finds its way to the surface.

THE SEA BREEZE

Any onshore wind (blowing in from the sea) is usually termed a "sea breeze." Because most days are windier in the afternoon, it is not always possible to determine what is a sea breeze and what is either a change in the synoptic situation or an enhancement of the gradient wind. Understanding the differences between an onshore wind and a true sea breeze, however, will help to plan the day's sail, and will greatly improve your chances on the race course.

In some form or another, the sea breeze can be found during spring and summer throughout the world. It can be a regular feature like the Fremantle Doctor of Western Australia or the afternoon breeze that makes for a perfect regatta. The sea breeze mechanism is not however confined to the sea; *lake breezes* on any large body of water are likely. In mountainous regions a mountain and valley wind regime is sometimes experienced as the wind drains down the valley at night only to reverse in direction during the late morning and afternoon.

CONDITIONS NECESSARY FOR A SEA BREEZE

The sea breeze (in theory) will start near the shore and blow at right angles to it. As the day progresses it will keep extending offshore, strengthen, and veer (or back in the Southern Hemisphere), eventually blowing at about 20 degrees to the coast. It can reach some 20 miles out to sea and penetrate considerably more inland, but as no shoreline is straight, no sea breeze adheres strictly to the rules.

The sea breeze will be accelerated around headlands and funneled by the land. This can create a sea breeze that can reach 20 or even 25 knots in places, but in general the speeds are rather less. The topography of the land behind the coast is important, as steep barren mountains will heat more quickly than vegetated fields. The sea breeze, although possible to predict, varies greatly depending on locality.

It is the atmospheric pressure differential over land and sea that generates a sea breeze. As the land heats up air and moisture rise and expand causing the surface pressure over the land to fall. The rising and expanding air moves over the water, helped if there is an offshore breeze, and we now have higher pressure over the ocean than over the land. Air at the surface moves from the high to low pressure and our sea breeze circulation begins (see diagrams on page 64).

So we know the surface pressure differential between the land and sea, created by the heating effect of the land, starts the sea breeze off. We have also seen that an offshore component to the wind helps to get the circulation going.

If we have high pressure over the land and lower pressure over the sea, determined by using Buys Ballot's Law (see page 25) or by studying the charts, the chance of a sea breeze diminishes. This is because the pressure differential has to be reversed before it is possible to get the circulation going. This will normally cause the wind to drop as the pressure equalizes, with only a late, light sea breeze developing—if one develops at all.

Wind through a Typical Sea-Breeze Day

Light offshore wind in the early morning.

A period of calm, mid-morning, starting close to the beach.

An onshore wind develops near the coast.

The band of onshore wind rolls seaward but remains strongest near the land.

The wind veers as the afternoon progresses (backs in Southern Hemisphere).

Maximum wind speed mid to late afternoon.

THE CLOUDS THROUGH A SEA BREEZE

As we need convection for sea breezes to develop, we can expect cumulus clouds to appear. The earlier we start to see them develop, the earlier a sea breeze is likely to start. A clear patch of sky over the water with the clouds lining up on the land side of the coastline is often the first sign of the sea breeze.

Development of a Sea Breeze

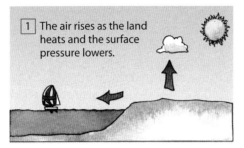

1 The air rises as the land heats and the surface pressure lowers.

1. The land must heat up to a greater temperature than the seawater—hence the best sea breezes are in the spring when the water temperature is at its coolest and in the summer when the land heats up the most. Local land radio broadcasts give expected temperatures.

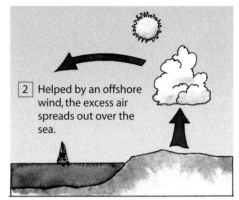

2 Helped by an offshore wind, the excess air spreads out over the sea.

2. There needs to be a light gradient wind that has an offshore component to it; 15 knots is generally considered the maximum gradient wind for the sea breeze to overcome. The greater the temperature contrast between land and sea, the higher the offshore wind the sea breeze can overcome.

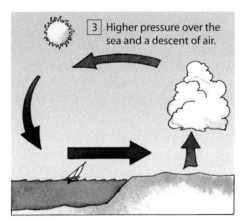

3 Higher pressure over the sea and a descent of air.

3. A difficult one to define, convection is needed to get the circulation going and can be seen by cumulus clouds forming. There needs to be convection, but only to a moderate level. Too much convection, producing towering cumulus clouds, showers, and possibly thunderstorms, can kill the sea breeze. Not enough, which can be the case during high pressure, and no matter how hot the land becomes, a sea breeze will struggle to develop.

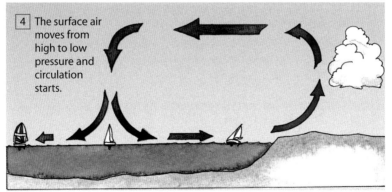

4 The surface air moves from high to low pressure and circulation starts.

4. The sea breeze develops as the land heats, which in turn causes the pressure to fall. The excess rising air drifts out over the sea—a light offshore gradient wind helps in this, increasing the pressure differential. Slightly higher pressure over the sea and lower over the land starts a circulation, as the surface air moves from high to low pressure.

A sea-breeze day with clouds over the land. (Helen Tibbs)

As the sea breeze develops, the cloud front moves inland and the clear area extends seaward. This is one reason why seaside resorts tend to be the sunniest places, as sea breezes move the clouds away, while only a few miles inland the clouds develop. We are even luckier sailing in coastal waters, looking at clouds over the land while sailing in clear skies.

Sea-Breeze Criteria

The land must become warmer than the sea.

There must be a light offshore component to the wind—less than 15 knots (unless a strong temperature contrast develops).

Slack pressure gradient.

There must be convection, i.e., cumulus clouds must be forming.

Expect 10–15 knots although a good sea breeze can reach 25 knots in places.

NOT QUITE A SEA BREEZE

Onshore gradient winds will often strengthen during the late morning and afternoon by 5–10 knots. This is caused as the land heats and the pressure falls. This is not a sea breeze but a thermally enhanced gradient wind. Picky perhaps, but it has important differences:

- There will not be a period of calm before the wind increases.
- The wind is unlikely to veer (in fact it may back as the pressure over the land falls).
- The cloud pattern is different.
- The clouds may not clear over the sea as there is no circulation bringing descending cooler air to clear them.

Clouds building over the mainland shore. (Helen Tibbs)

If the onshore gradient wind is from a direction that implies higher pressure over the land, then the wind is likely to drop during the day, however hot it becomes over the land.

ISLANDS AND INLAND WATERS

Islands generate their own sea breezes. Small islands close to the coast will be overwhelmed by the sea breeze generated by the larger landmass, although initially an island sea breeze may develop. Waters like the Chesapeake Bay have complex sea-breeze patterns. What starts as a sea breeze onto all the coasts around the bay may change to an ocean sea breeze across the whole bay funneling into the bays and rivers on the western shore. This gives different wind strengths and directions to places just a few miles apart.

At Cowes in England, on the Solent, the water between the Isle of Wight and the mainland (where major regattas are held), an interesting sight sometimes occurs. The sea breeze comes around the island and spinnakers can be seen approaching from the west and the east only to meet in the middle in an area of no wind. Usually, but not always, the southwesterly sea breeze eventually dominates the whole area.

On larger islands, sea breezes may form on all coasts. This makes it hard to find afternoon anchorages, as all coasts become lee shores, and as the wind blows strongest near the land, bays that might be expected to be sheltered are not.

With any island or peninsula, sea breezes that meet from different coasts give a *convergence* zone, where the only direction for the air and moisture to go is upward. This gives towering clouds and showers inland where they meet, often enhanced by hills or mountains. (See below for more on convergence.)

OTHER FACTORS AFFECTING COASTAL AREAS

The opposite of sea breezes, offshore night breezes are more influenced by topography than anything else. The air cools and drains by gravity to the sea, so the strongest night breezes can be expected opposite valleys and estuaries. These winds can be very localized and, near mountains, are as regular as a sea breeze.

It can be argued that a reverse circulation to the sea breeze is created, but this will only give a very light land breeze, the main effect being to bring the cold stable air off the land and over coastal waters, resulting in mainly calm conditions.

Katabatic winds are cold mountain winds blowing down valleys, which may spill over to the coast. They are driven by gravity and in high latitudes reach gale force or stronger. (*Anabatic* winds are the opposite, driven by rapid heating of rocky mountains creating circulation.) If sailing at night near mountainous regions, particularly if they are snow-capped, expect strong, cold, blasts of wind. Lake sailors are familiar with both katabatic and anabatic winds.

Sailing near the coast we find bands of wind that change considerably in both strength and direction. It is a rare day indeed when the wind is steady, and this is generally only when it blows directly onto the shore.

Stability is one reason why there are gusts and lulls. Although we have looked in detail at how the stability changes over land due to the changing temperature, we must also look at the different air masses and how stability affects them.

The changes along the coast are often greater than explained before and are due to mechanical forces as the wind flows over, and around, obstructions seeking a path of least resistance. There are also effects due to coastal *divergence* and convergence.

Most coastlines change direction with bays and headlands, estuaries and islands, making it necessary to look at the principles of how the wind is changed by the coastline.

Some features will affect the wind for many miles downwind, while others last for just a few hundred yards. The effect of funneling is an example where the wind increase lasts for many miles.

Between two large landmasses the wind will accelerate to strong or gale force, even when general winds are moderate. The best example of this is through the Straits of Gibraltar; the wind is bent and accelerated by the high mountains to the north and south. This funnels the wind, making entering or leaving the Mediterranean difficult. This has, however, put the town of Tarifa on the windsurfing map!

But we do not have to go so far from home to find examples of wind accelerating through gaps. The previously mentioned Santa Ana wind in southern California accelerates through canyons sometimes causing damage on land and difficult conditions at sea.

(Chris Tibbs)

On a smaller scale, the wind is often accelerated at the entrance of a river or estuary although all around the wind is light. This can make mooring and maneuvering difficult with the strongest wind found all day through the marina and in the river. This is made worse the deeper the river valley is and the higher the hills. The wind here may have little in common in direction or strength to that found a few miles out to sea.

OFFSHORE WINDS

When the wind blows from the land to the sea it is said to be offshore.

Friction slows and backs the wind to a greater extent over the land than the sea. It therefore follows that as the wind leaves the land it veers and accelerates.

As a guide, the wind will veer about 15 degrees and increase considerably, sometimes doubling in speed after it has left the land.

The effect of the wind increasing as it moves away from the land is most noticeable in the first few hundred yards but it can continue for several miles out to sea. Few coastlines are uniform, so the wind will funnel down any valleys, creating bands of stronger, gustier wind that extend out to sea.

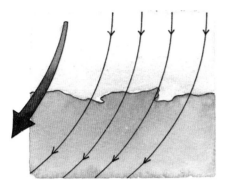

The wind veers and accelerates as it leaves the land.

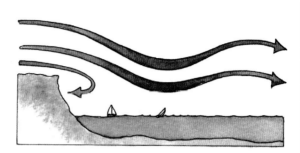

Wind blowing over cliffs will produce eddies near the cliffs and bands of stronger and lighter winds farther away.

This makes it difficult to predict the wind at sea from the security of a sheltered marina.

The bend in the wind as it leaves the land can be used to advantage, as a steady lift can be expected on port tack when beating toward the land, as well as a decrease in the wind. However, because of the shape of the land, this effect will not always be experienced. It has also been argued that a large temperature contrast between the land and the sea will change the stability of the air enough to mask this effect, and could in fact reverse it.

Wind coming off the land over cliffs can give unexpected patterns. Close to high cliffs, eddies can form in the wind flow, giving a reversal of direction, as shown in the accompanying illustration. The wind beyond this is then often strongly banded as the air forms a wave, giving stronger wind as it reaches the surface. Known as *lee waves*, they can also be found wherever mountains lie across the flow. Sometimes *lenticular clouds* form at the top of these waves in the air—looking a little like flying saucers, these clouds can be spectacular if lit by the setting sun.

WIND BLOWING PARALLEL TO THE SHORELINE

When the wind is blowing parallel to the shore, the wind over the land is backed with relation to the wind over the sea. Consequently, on a straight coast the wind over the land bends either toward the wind over the sea (convergence) or away from it (divergence).

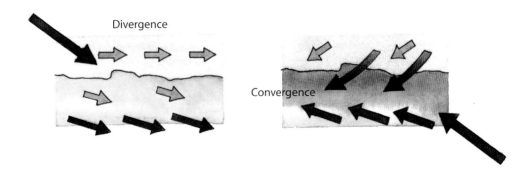

If the land is on the starboard side of a boat running with the wind astern, the wind will be converging so, for a band of up to two or three miles from the coast, the wind will be strengthened by a few knots—perhaps as much as 25 percent.

If the land is on the port side of a boat running with the wind astern, the wind will be diverging, so the wind will generally be lighter along the coast.

> When sailing near the coast with the wind blowing parallel to the land:
> With the wind on your back, land on your left, expect less wind.
> With the wind on your back, land on your right, expect stronger winds.

No coastline is straight and the wind is rarely parallel to it, so the effects are not uniform. Bands of stronger and lighter winds may extend a couple of miles out to sea but there are no hard and fast rules. The biggest help is in knowing whether the wind is likely to increase or decrease when approaching the coast, so that sail selection can be made in good time.

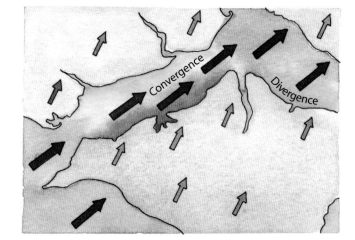

Convergence and divergence in a strait. Areas of convergence are shown by red shading and divergence by a lighter blue color. The darker the wind arrows the stronger the wind.

HEADLANDS

Any headland jutting out into the flow of wind will funnel and bend the wind around it. There will be an area of acceleration where the wind flows come together (convergence) and a fanning out of the wind behind the headland (divergence). The terms are the same as when talking about coastal convergence. When headland convergence and coastal convergence work together, the wind may increase substantially. If the headland is high, lee eddies may form along with gusts and lulls.

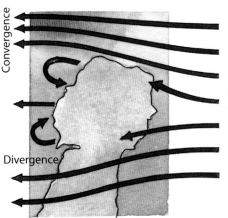

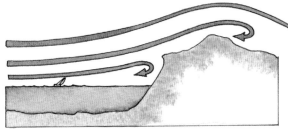

Wind lifts off the surface of the water giving disturbed light wind close to the cliffs.

Wind around a headland. Convergence is shown by the red shading and divergence is shown where the arrows move apart, indicating lighter winds.

If the headland is on a convergent coastline, then the increase of wind around the headland will be greater, as the backing wind passing over the land will add to the wind increase. No two headlands are the same and a small change in the wind direction may make a big difference, as does the actual shape and height of the land.

On a divergence coast, the lighter band of wind will be expected close in, and although there is likely to be an increase in wind around the headlands due to funneling, the overall increase should be less than on a convergent coastline.

A side effect of convergence and divergence is in the amount of cloud. Converging airstreams create an ascent of air and will create clouds, while diverging airstreams create descent and less cloud.

ONSHORE

With the wind blowing directly onto the land, there are few effects felt out on the water as the changes in the wind occur over and around the land. However, close to cliffs or high obstacles on the coast, the wind will lift off the surface leaving an area of fluky wind close inshore (see illustration). There can also be a change in the wind near headlands jutting out into the flow. Wind bands will be stronger either side of the headland as the flow of wind is divided by the land.

ISLAND IN THE FLOW

The divergence and convergence argument can be taken further and applied to islands. An island in the flow will have a windy side and a calmer side depending on the wind's direction.

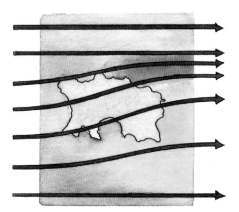

Convergence by an island showing a windy side and a calmer side.

The Canary Islands are well known for funneling and convergence zones. The high islands disturb the flow, as shown by the cloud patterns. (NASA/GSFC MODIS Rapid Response Project)

The height of the island will also have an affect, creating gusts and lulls. The accompanying drawing shows a band of stronger wind, which in reality will not be as clear-cut as the diagram suggests.

The land effects, whether mechanical, thermal, or a mixture of both, help to explain why the wind that we are actually sailing in can be quite different from that which was suggested by a wide-area forecast. No forecast can take into account the local variations in the wind that can be found just a few miles, if not yards, apart. Predicting local variations is not only interesting to do, it will also add to your enjoyment of being on the water.

CHAPTER 9

Weather at Sea

Once we are away from the influence of the land, the winds will be more like those we might expect from the synoptic chart. This does not, however, mean that the wind will be steady in either direction or strength; there are still likely to be bands of wind of varying strength.

Once we decide to head out to sea, there is still the need to look at the forecasts to see the overall synoptic picture before refining it for the area we are sailing in. We need to know how the wind is likely to behave in both the short and long term:

Short term—to decide which sails to use and the conditions to prepare for.
Long term—to position the boat to take advantage of any wind swings or to avoid, if possible, strong winds.

Although it is thought to be the preserve of single-handed ocean races or merchant shipping, we all *weather route* to some extent whenever we leave harbor. Heading up a few degrees in case we get headed when making for an entrance, or deciding what port to head for, is all weather routing, just on a less grand scale than having a weather forecaster send directions.

Away from land, on a long crossing, there is greater flexibility in our course and it may be worth sailing extra miles to stay with favorable winds.

PLANNING

While we are still in the planning stage ashore, synoptic charts can be downloaded from the Internet, received by fax, or found on notice boards in marinas. (See Weather Briefing Packages on page 141.)

Trade wind sailing. (Helen Tibbs)

Synoptic charts are our basic tools and we can add to them in a number of ways, particularly if we have Internet or e-mail capabilities.

The analysis of synoptic charts brings together the theory of synoptic scale systems and the likely cloud and weather to be expected. We have seen how to measure the wind speed from the chart and modify it for the drag of the surface. We should add our current observations to confirm that what should be happening and what is happening are the same.

WEATHER ROUTING AT SEA

All the time we are adding to the puzzle to understand what is happening, in a meteorological sense, so that we can forecast the most likely changes and use them to our advantage. Knowing if the wind is going to change in direction or strength allows us to head off on the most favorable tack.

Over the open ocean, without the influence of land, there are still localized changes to be expected in the wind. These will be mainly associated with clouds or a change in water temperature.

Large changes in water temperature are linked to main ocean currents, and are well documented in Sailing Directions (Pilots) and on Pilot or Routing charts. Pilot charts give average monthly meteorological conditions to be found over an ocean and include major currents.

Ocean currents are important as they move cold or warm water around the globe and help to regulate climate; the water modifies the temperature and humidity of the air above it. The boundaries between warm and cold water are often places of significant meteorological events where cyclogenesis (development of lows), fog, and thunderstorms are likely. Examples of this are the warm Gulf Stream along the East Coast and the cold *California Current* of the West Coast.

Some of these features are discussed further in Chapter 10 (Meteorological Dangers) and Chapter 14 (Around the World).

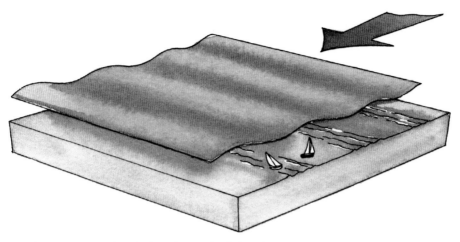

Over the open ocean, the wind tends to arrive in bands.

The boundary between warm and cold water will also divide air of different stability. The warm water heats the air making it more unstable, and the circulation brings more air from above the boundary layer, reducing drag and increasing the average wind speed.

There will also be more gusts and lulls with the wind veering and backing a few degrees as each gust passes. If this sounds familiar it is because the boundary between the water temperatures acts like a coastline, with slower backed wind over the colder water, and stronger veered wind over the warm.

Wind Lanes

Over open water, particularly in the trade wind belts, fair weather cumulus clouds often form in well-defined bands, or lanes, with clear sky between each lane. Cumulus clouds are

a sign of ascending air, so under each line of cloud there is likely to be a band of relatively light winds, where the surface air is rising.

The clear bands, by contrast, are a sign of descending air. The air aloft is usually moving faster than the surface wind, so when it drops to surface level it will be felt as an increase in the wind strength. When it reaches the surface it can fall no farther, of course, so it moves horizontally to replace the air that has been drawn upward under the clouds. Where this horizontal movement is in the same direction as the gradient wind, they combine to produce a band of wind that is stronger still.

The whole pattern of alternating bands of strong and light winds tends to move as though it were being blown along by the gradient wind. This means that if you are trying to stay in the strongest wind, it is better to sail through the lulls on port tack, in order to reach the next clear band as quickly as possible, and then to tack onto starboard in order to stay with it.

Any change in the clouds is significant and needs to be identified and fitted into the synoptic situation. Small-scale features will not be included in the synoptic charts, as they are too small to be represented but they are still significant to sailors. These small-scale features include thunderstorms and squalls which can add significantly to the wind strength.

Away from the land the wind will behave as we would expect from the synoptic charts rather than changing direction and strength every few miles that tends to happen when sailing along a coast. We need to keep a weather eye for changes in the clouds, as they will herald a change in the wind. Offshore forecasts—a term that usually describes forecasts for more than 25 miles offshore—are for large areas of ocean and there may be considerable differences in wind strength from one part of the forecast area to another. Sometimes when sailing downwind of mountain ranges we get a sudden increase in wind even though we are well out of the sight of the land. This can be caused by waves in the atmosphere rising over the mountains and coming in a rush down to the surface of the sea—so even well away from the land, land influences can extend for a considerable distance.

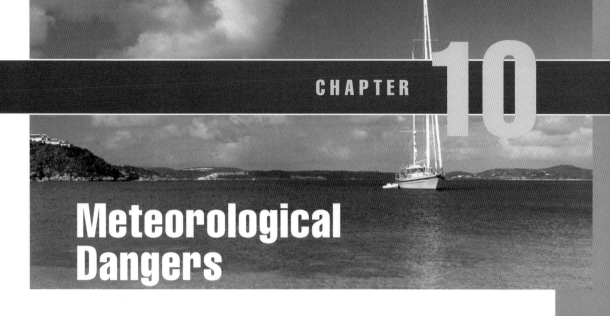

CHAPTER 10

Meteorological Dangers

From novice crew to superyacht captains, one of our biggest worries is getting caught out in bad weather. At some time in our sailing career we are likely to find ourselves in conditions that we would rather not be in.

GALES

Gales do not arrive without any warning at all, but sometimes conditions may deteriorate more than expected. One of the best instruments to help forewarn us of deteriorating conditions, but one that is often overlooked in our high-tech world, is the barometer. There may be local conditions that accelerate the wind (see Chapter 9) but when a gale develops it is invariably preceded by a change in pressure. This change need not be a fall: as the old saying goes, a quick rise after low predicts a stronger blow.

(Chris Tibbs)

As a rule of thumb, a change of 5 or 6mb in three hours predicts a Force 6 (22–27 knots), while a change of 8mb foretells a Force 8 (34–40 knots). This is only a guide, as a lot depends on the wind we have as our starting point. If it is already blowing Force 6 or 7 and the barometer is dropping quickly, then a gale is imminent. If we are starting at a lower wind strength, we have a bit more time to prepare. The same is true with a quick rise in pressure—any steep pressure gradient indicates strong winds.

In many lows, the tightest isobars, and hence the strongest winds, are found on the back (northwesterly side) of the low after a cold front. If the low is moving in the customary way of west to east, the stronger wind soon passes.

If, in the warm sector of a low, the barometer is still falling, the low is either deepening or moving closer—in either case expect stronger winds.

SECONDARY LOWS

Secondary lows (see also Chapter 5) can develop in the circulation of a main depression, with pressure dropping quickly as the secondary low intensifies to become deeper than the primary. This rapid deepening is sometimes described as a *bomb* or "explosive" cyclogenesis and normally only happens if the secondary low develops more than 600 miles from its parent.

The strongest wind will be on the side away from the original low. The first signs on a synoptic chart are the widening of the isobars before successive charts show circulation developing and a deepening of central pressure. On satellite pictures, a comma-shaped cloud develops and this can be the first real sign that the low is deepening quickly.

GUSTS

Gusts are rapid but short-lived increases in wind. The opposite of gusts are the lulls that accompany them. There are a number of reasons why gusts occur; if the wind is blowing off the land they are probably of a turbulent nature caused by obstructions to the wind on the land. In an onshore wind, they are more likely to be caused by vertical movement in the atmosphere and are likely to be strongest on a day when the atmosphere is unstable. This is indicated by large cumulus clouds: the greater the vertical extent, the gustier the conditions.

Gusts caused by instability of the atmosphere may increase the wind by 30–50 percent and are thought by many sailors to veer the wind. There seems to be little scientific evidence to support this and whether the change in direction is a veer or a back in the wind direction will depend which side of a cloud we are on.

Boat broaching. Gusts can catch even professional sailors out. (Rick Tomlinson)

Gusts generated by turbulence over land can increase the wind strength even more, sometimes as much as doubling the average.

SQUALLS

A gust becomes a squall if it lasts longer than a minute and involves a wind speed at least 16 knots higher than the mean, and exceeds 22 knots. It is obviously a significant event and potentially dangerous. The warning signs are usually rain or hail, and a big dark cloud.

The term "squall line" was originally used to describe a cold front—it is a good description. Cold fronts, or troughs, can be seen approaching with towering cumulus clouds and heavy rain. Expect squall lines to back the wind slightly as they approach and the wind to veer once the clouds pass.

Squalls are common in the unstable air behind cold fronts, particularly if the air is very cold. If there is precipitation falling from a big cumulus cloud, expect the worst and reef early.

Squall clouds have their own circulation similar to that for a cumulus cloud. They are much bigger, reaching to great heights and are steered by the wind blowing at a much higher level. They are similar to the thunderstorms described below.

Not all large black clouds have squalls attached and it is sometimes difficult to know which will produce a squall and which will just give a small short-lived gust. Rain is a good indication; the heavier the rainfall, the stronger the squall is likely to be.

THUNDERSTORMS

Thunderstorms are not only dramatic but can also be dangerous. There is the danger of being struck by lightning (luckily, this only happens rarely) but there is also the risk of a strong gust of wind ahead of the storm arriving with gale force ferocity along with stinging rain and hail.

This squall is sweeping down a valley and over the sea.
(Bluegreen Pictures)

Circulation in a thunderstorm.

Thunderstorms are caused by instability in the atmosphere, with overheated air near the surface and much cooler air above. This shows itself as towering cumulus clouds—which may or may not have the classic "anvil-shaped" head described in many textbooks. As the clouds grow, a thunderstorm, or at least a heavy squall, is possible.

The gust is short-lived but potentially damaging in its violence and, as it arrives quickly, gives little time to shorten sail. It soon gives way to heavy rain and a dropping wind. Ahead of the gust front the wind will ease and as the gust front arrives will change direction depending on which side of the storm cloud you are on.

Thunderstorms reach up to the tropopause, which may be 40,000 feet (12km) above our heads. The wispy anvil top that is sometimes seen is ice crystals blowing in the jet stream at that height. Because of the vertical extent of the clouds, the movement of the storm follows the winds high up. This may be very different from the direction of the wind that you are sailing in so the track of a thunderstorm or big squall may be difficult to predict and requires close monitoring.

In mid-latitudes thunderstorms at sea are relatively rare; however, in some places in the tropics and subtropics (e.g., Florida), they can be an almost daily occurrence in the hot season. Thunderstorms are driven by heat and they mainly form over the land late in the afternoon. They are sometimes referred to as "air mass" or "ordinary" thunderstorms. Occasionally a large supercell storm forms and this can maintain itself as a single entity for a number of hours, becoming extremely powerful. They can have downdrafts of well over gale force accompanied by hailstones greater than two inches in diameter. For inland sailors

Cumulonimbus (thunder) clouds. (Chris Tibbs)

on lakes and rivers, these storms can become a problem and it is worth monitoring the weather radio to listen for the chance of thunderstorms. In addition, the rainfall of these storms can cause flash flooding many miles from the actual storm.

One of the first times I was caught in a thunderstorm was while sailing on the Chesapeake Bay many years ago. The sky darkened and the skipper immediately ordered all sails taken off. Shortly afterward the gust front hit with great ferocity; the last sight of a boat still sailing was of flogging sails and the boat heeled at an alarming angle. Visibility was then reduced to a few yards. The strong wind was short-lived and we were soon sailing again.

Altocumulus castellanus are a sign of thundery weather. As the name suggests they are lumpy clouds that reach high into the atmosphere and look (loosely) like castle ramparts in the air.

We may also get frontal thunderstorms associated with cold fronts. Whereas most thunderstorms occur late in the afternoon when the land is at its warmest, frontal thunderstorms can happen at any time of the day or night and move as part of the cold front. The thunderstorms are usually right along the cold front; however, occasionally a squall line forms ahead of the front. This may be 60–180 miles (100–300km) ahead of the front in a severe squall line giving heavy rain or hail and strong squall winds.

There are Internet sites that show daily lightning strikes, known as *sferics*, and it is quite interesting to see where the thunderstorms commonly occur. (See Weather Websites on page 146.)

Thunder, incidentally, is the sound produced by lightning, and they happen at precisely the same moment. The reason thunder is usually heard after lightning is because sound travels more slowly than light. As a rule of thumb, the time difference between lightning and thunder is about six seconds per nautical mile. This is a good way to monitor the progress of a storm.

TORNADOES

Tornadoes are rapidly rotating winds that blow around a small area of intense low pressure. They can occur in any state although the majority occur through the Central Plains extending from Texas to Nebraska, an area that has been dubbed "tornado alley." March to July is the most likely time for tornado activity but they can occur any time of year.

Although relatively small, generally in the region of 300–2,000 feet (100–600 meters) in diameter, tornadoes can pack a powerful punch with wind speeds exceeding 200 knots in the more powerful ones. They typically move at 20–40 knots and last for just a few minutes with an average path length of around four miles. The devastation that tornadoes cause can be immense and is a combination of the very strong wind and low pressure.

Tornadoes form over the land and are associated with severe thunderstorms. They sometimes form in families from the same supercell thunderstorm, at other times along an active cold front. As they form over the land they are not likely to affect sailors at sea, but for sailors on inland waters, the track could pass close by, or even over, lakes and rivers; these are called tornadic *waterspouts*. Tornadoes may also form in the eye wall of a hurricane.

Tornado tracks are erratic; it is impossible to predict whether any particular location will be hit or missed. However, the forecasts will give an indication as to whether or not conditions are favorable for their formation. There needs to be an unstable atmosphere with warm moist air near the surface and cold dry air at height—the same conditions as for severe thunderstorms. Due to the destructive power of a tornado, and the loss of life they inflict, local radio forecasts keep the public informed of any developments.

WATERSPOUTS

Out at sea we are much more likely to meet a waterspout, the smaller cousin of the tornado. Although a tornadic waterspout (a waterspout that starts life as a tornado over land) can be as destructive as a tornado, the majority of waterspouts are much smaller than the average tornado in size and ferocity. Typically they have diameters between 10 and 300 feet (3–100 meters) and have winds up to 45 knots. They may last 10–15 minutes and their forward movement is usually slow.

Waterspouts are more common in the tropics and subtropics but any large body of warm water can spawn them. They frequently form over the Great Lakes in summer. Florida has the highest number of recorded waterspouts; they are sometimes referred to as "fair weather" waterspouts.

Although some instability in the atmosphere is necessary, there does not need to be as much as that necessary for supercell thunderstorms and tornado development on land. They form mainly over warm shallow waters when large cumulus or cumulonimbus clouds are forming. There is an indication that some convergence—maybe from opposing sea breezes or gust fronts—will trigger a waterspout if other conditions are present.

The funnel of a waterspout is condensed water vapor and although spray may be lifted into the air by a few feet where the funnel touches down on the water, there is no lifting of

Multiple waterspouts near the Bahamas. (NOAA)

water into the core of the waterspout. The funnel extends from underneath a cloud toward the water and this may be met by a cone lifting from the surface. The waterspout will roughly follow the course of the parent cloud; after a while the core breaks and the funnel lifts back into the cloud.

Eyewitness accounts of yachts caught in a waterspout tell of being spun around with little control, and the whole experience being over quickly. Their advice is to take down all sails and motor away from the expected track of the waterspout if possible.

FOG

There are two main types of fog found at sea and around the coasts—advection and radiation fog. Both are caused by the air cooling until the dew point is reached.

ADVECTION FOG

Advection fog is the true sea fog caused by warm moist air moving over cold water. The cold water cools the lowest layer of the air to such an extent that the water vapor in the air condenses to form droplets of liquid water. The air temperature at which this occurs is known as the dew point.

Around the coast of the U.S. advection fog is common in spring or early summer when the seawater is cool and warm moist air moves over it. There must be light winds to move the air over the water but once the wind speed reaches around 15 knots, the fog lifts off the water and forms low stratus clouds.

This type of fog can last for long periods of time, often until there is a change in the air mass. There are some well-documented fog banks that form quickly when certain conditions prevail. The best known are the fog banks over the Grand Banks off Newfoundland, where cold water is brought south by the Labrador Current and warm moist air moves north with the Gulf Stream. Although theory tells us that with more than about 15 knots

(Chris Tibbs)

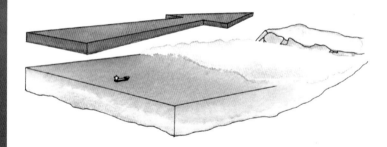

Warm moist air passing over a cold sea produces advection fog.

Radiation fog drifting down to the sea.

of wind the fog lifts off the surface to form low stratus cloud, I have been on the Grand Banks with 25 knots of wind and thick fog!

The West Coast is also often plagued by fog through the summer as the Pacific High, along with the heating of the land, gives onshore winds. Warm moist air is drawn over the cool coastal waters—made cool by the southerly flowing California Current. The warm moist air and cool waters generate the fog banks that may last for several days.

Air with a dew point higher than the seawater temperature is likely to give widespread fog. If it is similar, the fog will be patchy as the temperature of the sea varies a little with the change of tides and upwelling. Measuring dew point is not something that we regularly do on board a yacht but we can find reports on the Internet from buoys and station circles. There are also an increasing number of buoy reports accessible via cell phone.

RADIATION FOG

Radiation fog is a land fog formed during clear nights under high pressure. Without any cloud cover to blanket the ground, the heat radiates upward and is lost to space. As the ground cools, the air above it cools. If the air temperature falls below the dew point, fog is formed.

Although this is a land fog, it drifts down rivers and estuaries and finds its way over coastal waters. As the fog drifts out over the relatively warm sea, the air is warmed and starts to rise, mixing with the air at higher levels. This combination of warming and mixing is the beginning of the breakup of the fog. The sun will warm the fog from above so over the open sea, radiation fog is quickly dispersed.

The coldest part of the night is around dawn; the hour after dawn can see the height of the radiation fog. The heating of the sun will, on all but the worst days, quickly burn the fog off and a strong wind will rapidly disperse it. A marina may be fog-bound in the early morning while out to sea it is clear.

Radiation fog is often the worst in the autumn and winter, when on land it is reluctant to shift all day. The cold water of rivers lowers the local sea temperature, allowing the fog to spread to coastal waters, particularly in areas such as the Great Lakes and any inland waterways.

Land forecasts report the chance of fog, as it is so important for drivers. However, any night with clear skies and light winds is likely to produce radiation fog.

Knowing the type of fog is important in deciding when it is likely to clear; advection fog may well last until there is a change in wind direction and weather system, while radiation fog needs heat to burn it off and is likely to be only near the coast and in rivers and estuaries.

WAVES

Waves are caused mainly by the wind, so their size depends mainly on the strength of the wind, on how long it has been blowing, and on its *fetch*—the uninterrupted distance that it has been blowing over water.

Over deep, open water, waves are likely to correspond reasonably well with the descriptions given in the Beaufort scale (see page 57). In coastal waters, however, the tidal stream

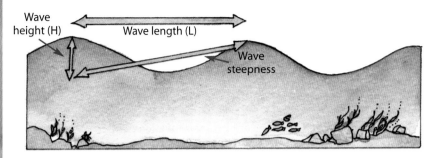

Idealized wave.

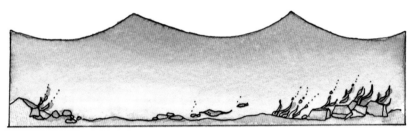

As waves grow they take on a more peaked shape.

Actual wave shapes from a wave recorder showing little symmetry.

Breaking waves are often found when the wind blows over tidal water in a narrow channel. (Helen Tibbs)

and depth of water play an important part, particularly affecting the shape and steepness of the waves.

If the tidal stream is against the wind, the wave length (the distance between crests) will shorten by as much as 50%. The wave height, however, will stay much the same, so the steepness of each wave will increase significantly, producing what is described as a "short, steep, sea."

When the average slope of a wave increases to about 1 in 7 (a height/length ratio of about 0.14) it is likely to break. This dissipates its energy, and may leave a short-lived patch of relatively calm water. While it is breaking, however, a wave is at its most dangerous: big breakers are easily capable of capsizing or pitchpoling yachts, or of smashing windows or superstructures. The 1998 Sydney–Hobart Race turned into a disaster because the wind, blowing against a strong ocean current, produced breaking waves large enough to cause knockdowns and inversions that claimed six lives.

Shallow water has a similar effect: when a wave runs into water that is shallower than about half its wavelength, the water movement in the lower levels of the wave is restricted by the seabed, so the whole wave has to slow down, shortening its wavelength, and making it steeper and more likely to break. This is why you often find waves breaking on a beach, and why harbors with shallow entrances or bars need to be treated with respect in onshore winds.

The effect will be particularly pronounced where headlands or narrow channels increase the speed of the tidal stream, or where a shallow and uneven seabed produces overfalls.

SQUEEZE ZONES

Where high pressure and low pressure move close together, we can get a zone where the isobars are squeezed together producing stronger winds. This can happen unexpectedly, if you're looking at a series of synoptic charts at 24-hour intervals: at each time step the low

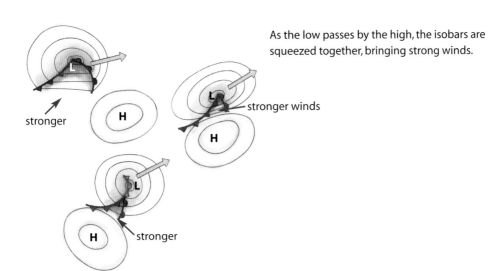

As the low passes by the high, the isobars are squeezed together, bringing strong winds.

High pressure and strong winds on the edge of a high-pressure system.
(Christian Fevier/Bluegreen Pictures)

and high may be well separated, but for the low to have got to the second position it will have passed close to the high. This is most likely to happen on the north side of high pressure in the Northern Hemisphere (south side in the Southern), where transient lows predominate.

MOUNTAINS

Wherever mountains interrupt the flow of wind there is likely to be an increase in pressure on the windward side and a drop in pressure on the leeward side—this is called lee troughing (see page 23). This is a purely mechanical process but it can create a strong flow

Anchorages near mountains can lead to uncomfortable nights.

around the sides of the mountains. The Mistral in the Mediterranean is probably the best-known wind of this type, but any range of mountains will have a similar effect on local wind conditions.

Wind coming over high hills and mountain ranges will accelerate through passes and down valleys (see illustration). In the lee of such mountains we can find very strong, gusty winds.

Cold katabatic wind from high up the mountain is also a possibility at night. These winds can be very localized making guides and pilot books an essential addition to cruising library.

Katabatic winds can reach storm force in high latitudes near snow- and ice-covered mountains.

WIND CHILL

Wind chill is the name given to the cooling effect of wind. In hot weather, of course, a "cooling breeze" is quite pleasant, though it can mask the early symptoms of developing sunburn. Early- and late-season sailors, however, need to be careful of the risk of developing hypothermia even if the actual air temperature is not particularly low.

Over the sea where temperatures are more moderate and we are used to measuring the wind in knots, and forecasts are for winds at a 10-meter height, the accompanying table may be of use. For example, for an air temperature of 50°F (10°C), the wind chill equivalent temperature is 36.5°F (2.5°C) in 20 knots of wind and 29.3°F (−1.5°C) in 40 knots. Of course a wet sailor will chill at a faster rate than a dry sailor.

Temperature (°F)																		
Wind (mph)	40	35	30	25	20	15	10	5	0	-5	-10	-15	-20	-25	-30	-35	-40	-45
5	36	31	25	19	13	7	1	-5	-11	-16	-22	-28	-34	-40	-46	-52	-57	-63
10	34	27	21	15	9	3	-4	-10	-16	-22	-28	-35	-41	-47	-53	-59	-66	-72
15	32	25	19	13	6	0	-7	-13	-19	-26	-32	-39	-45	-51	-58	-64	-71	-77
20	30	24	17	11	4	-2	-9	-15	-22	-29	-35	-42	-48	-55	-61	-68	-74	-81
25	29	23	16	9	3	-4	-11	-17	-24	-31	-37	-44	-51	-58	-64	-71	-78	-84
30	28	22	15	8	1	-5	-12	-19	-26	-33	-39	-46	-53	-60	-67	-73	-80	-87
35	28	21	14	7	0	-7	-14	-21	-27	-34	-41	-48	-55	-62	-69	-76	-82	-89
40	27	20	13	6	-1	-8	-15	-22	-29	-36	-43	-50	-57	-64	-71	-78	-84	-91
45	26	29	12	5	-2	-9	-16	-23	-30	-37	-44	-51	-58	-65	-72	-79	-86	-93
50	26	19	12	4	-3	-10	-17	-24	-31	-38	-45	-52	-60	-67	-74	-81	-88	-95
55	25	18	11	4	-3	-11	-18	-25	-32	-39	-46	-54	-61	-68	-75	-82	-89	-97
60	25	17	10	3	-4	-11	-19	-26	-33	-40	-48	-55	-62	-69	-76	-84	-91	-98

Frostbite Times   ▨ 30 minutes   ▨ 10 minutes   ☐ 5 minutes

A wind chill table like this one gives you an idea of the apparent temperature when radiational cooling due to wind is factored in. (National Weather Service)

Wind Chill Equivalent Temperatures

Temperature	10-meter High Winds (Knots)							
(C°/F°)	5	10	15	20	25	30	35	40
20/68	19/66.2	17.5/63	16/60.8	15/59	14/57.2	13.5/56.3	13/55.4	12/53.6
16/60.8	15/59	13/55.4	11.5/52.7	10/50	9/48.2	8/46.4	7.5/45.5	7/44.6
12/53.6	11/51.8	8.5/47.3	6.5/43.7	5/41	4/39.2	3/37.4	2/35.6	1.5/34.7
10/50	8.5/47.3	6.5/43.7	4.5/40.1	2.5/36.5	1.5/34.7	0/32	−0.5/31.1	−1.5/29.3
8/46.4	6.5/43.7	4/39.2	2/35.6	0/32	−1/30.2	−2.5/27.5	−3.5/25.7	−4/24.8
6/42.8	4.5/40.1	2/35.6	−0.5/31.1	−2.5/27.5	−3.6/25.52	−5.2/22.64	−6.3/20.66	−7/19.4
4/39.2	2.5/36.5	−0.5/31.1	−3/26.6	−5/23	−6.5/20.29	−8/17.6	−9/15.8	−10/14
2/35.6	0.5/32.9	−2.5/27.5	−5/23	−7.5/18.5	−9/15.8	−10.5/13.09	−12/10.39	−13/8.59
0/32	−1.5/29.3	−5/23	−7.5/18.5	−10/14	−12/10.39	−13/8.59	−14.5/5.89	−16/3.19

CHAPTER 11

Hurricanes

Tropical revolving storms are intense lows that mature into hurricanes when they generate winds in excess of 63 knots (Force 12)—sometimes up to 180 knots—accompanied by torrential rain. On land, they cause widespread damage and considerable loss of life, while at sea, the wind, waves, and rain take their toll on mariners.

Hurricanes are found around the world and in both hemispheres within a band between 5 and 20 degrees of latitude from the equator (although there have been exceptions). They occur mainly during the summer months—though there are variations both in the names applied to them and to the exact season.

In the Atlantic and eastern Pacific they are known as hurricanes; in the west Pacific they are known as typhoons; in the Indian Ocean they are cyclones; and in Western Australia they are sometimes known as willy-willy. Whatever the local names are they are all tropical cyclones.

(NOAA)

The main hurricane season is June to November in the Northern Hemisphere and from December to March in the Southern Hemisphere. In the Bay of Bengal and Arabian Sea the cyclone season is split, with cyclones most likely between April and June and between September and December.

How to Remember the Caribbean Hurricane Season

June, too soon.
July, stand by.
August, come she must.
September, remember.
October, all over.

Occasionally, however, hurricanes develop outside the usual season, so it is as well to be wary and to listen out for forecasts whenever you're sailing in tropical waters. Fortunately, the barometer, in such areas, tends to be steady, with just a regular daily rise and fall of a couple of millibars peaking at about 1000 and 2200 and reaching a minimum at about 0400 and 1600. Any pressure falling significantly outside this normal daily range needs to be regarded as a possible early warning of a storm or hurricane.

Four Main Conditions Required for a Hurricane to Develop

1. More than five degrees of latitude away from the equator: this is because the Coriolis force, which is essential to start the rotation of the storm, is zero at the equator itself.

2. The seawater temperature must be at least 79°F (26C°) to a depth of at least 200 feet (60m). In practice, this usually means the surface temperature must be nearer 82°F (28C°).

3. An unstable atmosphere allowing deep convection to great heights.

4. Some form of initial disturbance, often an easterly wave (see page 130).

As a hurricane develops, it forms a distinctive circular patch of very dense cloud, with a clear "eye" at the center. Within the eye itself, winds are generally light but the sea is very rough and confused, because around it, in the "eye wall," winds may be blowing at up to 180 knots. Wind speeds generally decrease toward the outer edge of the storm: winds of "hurricane force" (Force 12, or over 63 knots) are most likely to be within about 75 miles of the center, while the wind farther than 100 miles from the center is unlikely to be more than gale force (Force 8, or 34–40 knots). A young hurricane usually moves fairly slowly, and in a generally westerly direction, angled slightly away from the equator, and gradually picking up speed until one of two things happens: either it reaches land, or it recurves—swinging abruptly toward the pole and then to the east.

> Tropical storms go through a life cycle and only a few become full-blown hurricanes.
> - Tropical Disturbance—the birth of a potential hurricane. An area of convective clouds develops and becomes organized with the beginning of some surface circulation.
> - Tropical Low—the pressure drops as the wind increases up to 33 knots.
> - Tropical Storm—the wind is between 34 and 63 knots. This is sometimes split into moderate and severe tropical storms.
> - Hurricane—once the wind gets above 63 knots.

Once a hurricane reaches land, it loses access to the massive reserves of heat energy that are stored in the sea and quickly dies. If it recurves, it soon finds itself over cooler water, so it either dies for the same reason, or else becomes weaker and more diffuse, and turns into a relatively ordinary mid-latitude low.

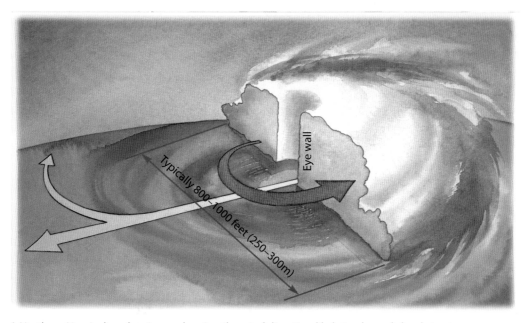

A Northern Hemisphere hurricane, showing the wind direction, likely tracks, and cloud structure.

Hurricanes are categorized using the *Saffir-Simpson Scale* from 1–5. Although Hurricane Katrina reached Category 5 intensity over the central Gulf of Mexico, it had weakened to a Category 3 before making landfall. The central pressure dropped to 902mb and although not quite the lowest on record it was a severe drop considering the standard or average pressure of 1013mb is used around the world. Deep Atlantic mid-latitude lows seldom fall below 975mb.

Hurricanes are named to help with identification, which is particularly useful if more than one hurricane is developing or active at any one time. For any named storm that causes extensive damage, or loss of life, the name is retired from the list.

The effect of wind spiraling around a moving center divides any hurricane into what are traditionally referred to as a "navigable semicircle" and a "dangerous semicircle." The diagram below shows the likely tracks of hurricanes and tropical storms in the different hemispheres. Although the winds within the storm are high, the speed of the storm itself is usually less than 15 knots, increasing as it moves out of the tropics. The usual track in the Northern Hemisphere is for the hurricane to travel in a west or northwesterly direction before curving more to the north over time and eventually the northeast. The dangerous semicircle is on the northerly side of this track; not only is it difficult to sail out of, as either tack tends to suck you in toward the center, but it is the side that the storm is most likely

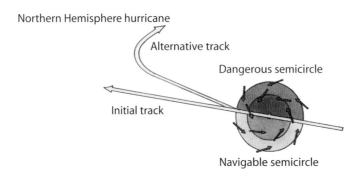

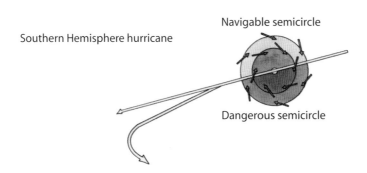

to turn toward. In the navigable semicircle, however, sailing on starboard tack will take you away from the center and away from the most likely track.

In the Southern Hemisphere our tactics are reversed as port takes us away from danger in the navigable semicircle.

Anywhere in the navigable semicircle of a Northern Hemisphere hurricane, broad reaching on starboard tack will take you away from the center and away from any possible recurvature. In the Southern Hemisphere, broad reaching on port tack will have the same effect.

In the dangerous semicircle of a Northern Hemisphere hurricane, port tack is definitely not an option: it will lead you straight toward the worst conditions. Starboard tack is little better: unless the hurricane has already passed you, it is only likely to prolong the agony by taking you parallel to the hurricane's track. If you are lucky enough to be able to make progress to windward under such conditions, you may just be able to escape to the north—where you will be ready to be caught by the same hurricane when it recurves!

Buys Ballot's Law (see page 25) shows you how to determine where you are in relation to the center of the hurricane: if you stand with your back to the wind in the Northern Hemisphere the center will be to your left. In most hurricane areas there are accurate hurricane forecasts that will give enough warning of a hurricane and its expected track to allow you time to either get out of its way or at least get across to the less dangerous side.

When I was caught in a hurricane, it was not clear-cut as to what the tactics should have been. Caught in the dangerous semicircle, the option of trying to cross the hurricane's track before it arrived was not appealing, but neither was staying where we were. In the end, the hurricane continued to curve to the east and passed some 70 miles to the north of our position, giving a very uncomfortable night with estimated wind speeds in excess of 90 knots for about 10 hours.

Torrential rain combined with the wind blowing the wave tops off prevented the boat from being overwhelmed, but at times it was touch and go. The overwhelming sensation though was one of intense noise. Dawn finally came and the wind eased a little at which stage the waves were at their most dangerous and sail was needed to get steerageway.

TYPICAL HURRICANE TRACKS NEAR THE U.S.

Predicting hurricanes is difficult and the tracks they take can be erratic. Historically hurricanes have affected the East Coast from the Gulf of Mexico to Cape Cod, with the more southerly regions bearing the brunt of the storms. In the Pacific, hurricanes develop to the west of Mexico and track toward the Northwest. As the track takes them over cooler water their power is much reduced and although Hawaii often looks to be on the track of a hurricane it is seldom hit—but the islands are not immune, and a number of hurricanes have hit Hawaii over the years.

With so much of the U.S. coast at risk from hurricanes, forecasts have become very accurate so the chance of getting caught out at sea is thankfully small. A major additional hazard along the coast is from the *storm surge*—a combination of higher water created by the low pressure and the amount of water being blown ashore. If this combines with high tides, flooding can be extensive. There is little the boater can do to protect the boat except take

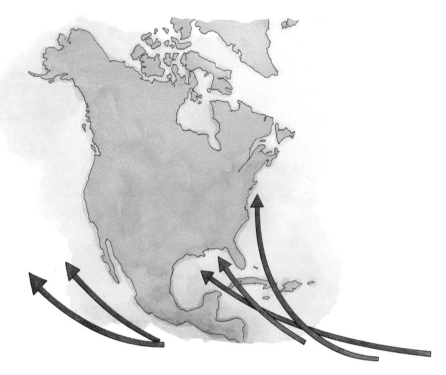

Typical hurricane tracks for North America—but note hurricane tracks can be erratic. (Christopher Hoyt)

everything possible down below, including all sails and covers, lash everything down, put out extra docking or mooring lines (with plenty of chafing gear), and evacuate the area with everyone else.

An increase in global temperatures may increase the intensity of storms, and there is observational evidence of increased intense tropical activity in the North Atlantic, although it is difficult to define long-term trends. There was a big jump in the number of recorded storms once we had routine satellite coverage of the area. However, there is big interannual variability; in 2006 there were very few named storms, while the previous year was the most active season on record. Some of the latest research however suggests that a change in the upper level winds from global warming will actually reduce the number of hurricanes in the future.

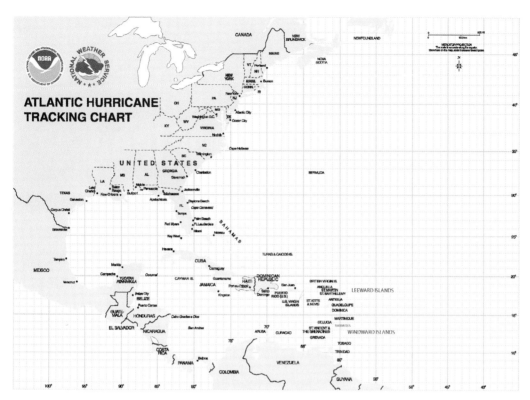

Blank hurricane tracking charts are available from the National Hurricane Center for the Atlantic and Pacific oceans at http://www.nhc.noaa.gov/. (National Hurricane Center)

CHAPTER 12

Putting It All Together

With virtually limitless sources of weather data readily available, it's easy to become overloaded with data and still not know what to do with it. The key is to understand and consider the data's reliability, and use it to synthesize a coherent picture before leaving shore.

The weather chart on page 99 shows lows and fronts that are not as neat as the diagrams in this book. Their structures will, however, be similar, and the conditions on the fronts will be as described. The wind may not veer on fronts as much as described in a textbook and the cloud structure may look jumbled up and difficult to identify, but the basics are the same and the more we understand, the safer and more enjoyable our sailing will be.

It is easy to get disillusioned by weather forecasts and claim that they never get it right. Sometimes this may be the case, but one area of disagreement between the forecast and the sailor is about what the forecast is trying to tell us, and what we are measuring and seeing.

Wind speed and direction in a forecast refer to an average wind speed over a five- or ten-minute period, measured at a height of 33 feet (10 meters). An anemometer (an instrument for measuring wind speed) on a mast higher than 33 feet will read a bit more, and on a shorter mast a bit less. On an average day, if there were such a thing, we can expect gusts to be a third as much again as forecast, and on an unstable day, with towering convective clouds, they may be higher still.

Forecasts refer to the true wind, yet while we are sailing our instruments generally display apparent wind (see sidebar). Add a tidal flow and the instruments may very well show two forces difference on the Beaufort scale (5–10 knots), between sailing upwind and running downwind. If you're estimating wind speed without instruments there is a tendency to overestimate light winds, and underestimate strong ones.

When sailing near the coast, mechanical and thermal effects of the land can have a significant impact on the wind strength. These effects are often very localized and are therefore unlikely to be included in any forecast. (See Chapter 8.)

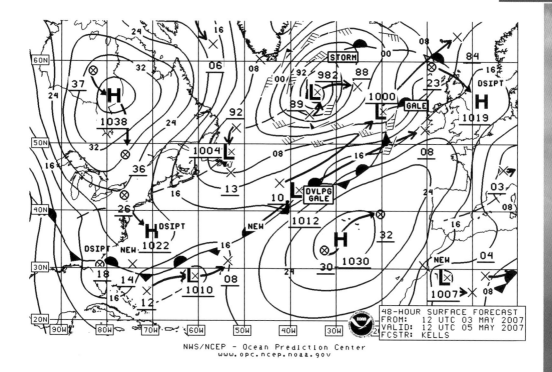

A 48-hour surface forecast chart for the Atlantic Ocean. (National Weather Service)

It is an interesting exercise to check buoy or coastal station reports after sailing (they are available on the Internet), and compare them to the winds that you have just experienced.

Apparent Wind

Apparent wind is the wind that we are sailing in, combining the true wind speed and our forward motion. If we were motoring directly into the wind, the apparent wind would be our speed through the water plus the true wind speed. At any time the apparent wind (the measured wind) is a combination of our forward motion through the water, the wind speed, and the tide or current. The only time the true and apparent wind are the same is when we are tied to a dock or at anchor (or on a mooring). The more sophisticated electronic instruments found on large boats or racing yachts give the option to display the apparent wind, or the true wind computed from the apparent (measured) wind, as well as the boat's heading and speed.

TYPES OF FORECASTS

In North America we have more weather forecasts available than anywhere else in the world. Through the National Weather Service (NWS), forecasts covering the oceans, coasts, and lakes as well as the land are all publicly available. In addition we have commercial companies providing specialist forecasts and a huge amount of information fed to us daily from the radio, newspapers, and even a dedicated weather channel, providing information 24/7. The biggest single source of weather information is, however, the Internet where forecasts and computer models can be found covering anywhere in the world. Most of this information is pure computer output and has little or no forecaster input interpreting it.

We will concentrate on the marine forecasts from the NWS as this covers our main sailing areas including the Great Lakes. These forecasts are readily available via radio so they can be received on the majority of vessels.

Sailing forecasts are split into three groups: Coastal, Offshore, and High Seas.

As their names suggest, the forecasts are geared to different users depending on distance from land. Most of our sailing is in bays and coastal waters around the country where the coastal forecast is of most importance as it (usually) extends from the coast to 25 miles offshore. For those venturing farther, offshore forecasts become most useful. However these are also useful for understanding what is happening on a greater scale than just the coastal area where we may be sailing. Like the distance that the coastal forecast extends offshore, the distances can vary between regions but usually cover 25 miles to 250 miles offshore.

High seas forecasts are geared more for large commercial vessels and emphasis is on gale and storm conditions. These forecasts are good for passagemaking and are used extensively by yachts heading to the Caribbean, Hawaii, or farther.

Forecasts have a logical and standard form, starting with the geographical area that they cover and when the forecast was issued. It will then continue with any warnings for the area. (These warnings are often set off in a special color if you are reading the forecast online.) These are strong wind and gale warnings (this may include or be a Small Craft Advisory); however, for (mainly) coastal areas, special warnings of potentially hazardous over-water events are also included. These may be short lived and can include thunderstorms, waterspouts, squalls, and major wind shifts. The equivalent land warnings will also be given if the event is expected to cross the coast.

Special Marine Warnings

Thunderstorms
Waterspouts
Squalls and major wind shifts

Once any warnings have been dealt with, the forecast continues with the synopsis. This tells us the movement of any large-scale weather systems. This is the movement of high-

or low-pressure systems, but the movement of fronts, troughs, or ridges likely to affect the area are also included.

Next come the actual conditions we can expect, the direction and speed of the wind given in compass points, and the speed in knots. The forecast will also include the likely height of waves, visibility, and a brief description of weather conditions. This is the likelihood of rain or showers and importantly any restrictions in visibility.

Rain can severely reduce visibility; moderate rain reduces visibility to 3–5 miles while heavy showers can reduce it to a few hundred yards. Pollution will reduce visibility still further.

Internationally, the meteorological definition of fog is for visibility to be less than 3280 feet (1000 meters). Drizzle is somewhere between fog and rain and is found in the warm sector of a low. Drizzle will significantly reduce visibility.

The forecast finishes with an outlook for the following days.

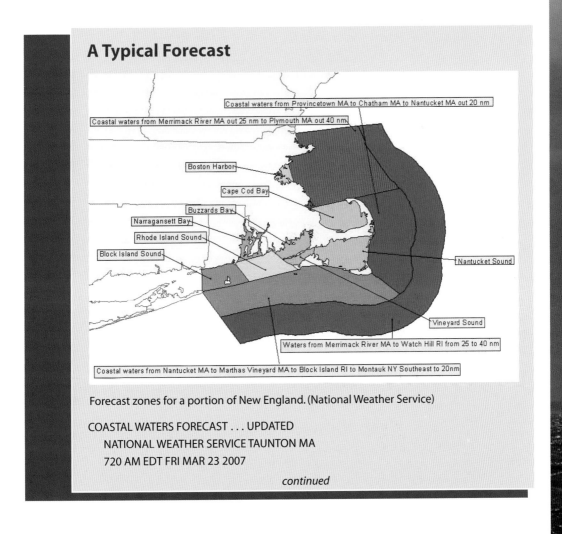

A Typical Forecast

Coastal waters from Provincetown MA to Chatham MA to Nantucket MA out 20 nm

Coastal waters from Merrimack River MA out 25 nm to Plymouth MA out 40 nm

Boston Harbor

Cape Cod Bay

Buzzards Bay

Narragansett Bay

Rhode Island Sound

Block Island Sound

Nantucket Sound

Vineyard Sound

Waters from Merrimack River MA to Watch Hill RI from 25 to 40 nm

Coastal waters from Nantucket MA to Marthas Vineyard MA to Block Island RI to Montauk NY Southeast to 20nm

Forecast zones for a portion of New England. (National Weather Service)

COASTAL WATERS FORECAST . . . UPDATED
NATIONAL WEATHER SERVICE TAUNTON MA
720 AM EDT FRI MAR 23 2007

continued

continued from previous

COASTAL WATERS FROM THE MERRIMACK RIVER MA TO WATCH HILL RI OUT TO 25 NM
ANZ200-232315-
720 AM EDT FRI MAR 23 2007
SYNOPSIS FOR MASSACHUSETTS AND RHODE ISLAND COASTAL WATERS
A COLD FRONT WILL SWEEP OFFSHORE EARLY THIS MORNING. HIGH PRES WILL THEN
BUILD OVER THE WATERS DURING TODAY INTO EARLY SAT. LOW PRES WILL PASS SOUTH
OF THE WATERS SAT NIGHT AND EARLY SUN. HIGH PRES THEN BUILDS ACROSS THE
WATERS ONCE AGAIN SUN NIGHT AND MON.
COASTAL WATERS FROM MERRIMACK RIVER MA OUT 25 NM TO PLYMOUTH MA OUT
40 NM . . . INCLUDING THE STELLWAGEN BANK NATIONAL MARINE SANCTUARY-
720 AM EDT FRI MAR 23 2007
TODAY
W WINDS 10 TO 15 KT. GUSTS UP TO 20 KT THIS MORNING. SEAS 2 TO 4 FT.
TONIGHT
NW WINDS 5 TO 10 KT . . . BECOMING N 10 TO 15 KT WITH GUSTS UP TO 20 KT AFTER
MIDNIGHT. SEAS 2 TO 3 FT.
SAT
NE WINDS 5 TO 10 KT . . . BECOMING E LATE. SEAS AROUND 2 FT.
SAT NIGHT
E WINDS 5 TO 10 KT. SEAS 1 FOOT OR LESS . . . THEN AROUND 2 FT AFTER MIDNIGHT. A
CHANCE OF RAIN AND SNOW SHOWERS AFTER MIDNIGHT WITH VSBY 1 NM OR LESS.
SUN
NE WINDS 10 TO 15 KT WITH GUSTS UP TO 20 KT. SEAS 2 TO 4 FT. A CHANCE OF SNOW
SHOWERS IN THE MORNING. VSBY 1 TO 3 NM.
SUN NIGHT
N WINDS 5 TO 10 KT . . . BECOMING NW LATE. SEAS 2 TO 3 FT.
MON
W WINDS 5 TO 10 KT . . . BECOMING S AFTER MIDNIGHT. SEAS 2 TO 4 FT.
TUE
SW WINDS 10 TO 15 KT. SEAS 2 TO 4 FT. A CHANCE OF SHOWERS.
THIS PRODUCT IS NORMALLY ISSUED TWICE DAILY AT APPROXIMATELY 4 AM AND 4
PM . . . AND UPDATED AS CONDITIONS WARRANT.

Hurricane and Tropical Storm Advisories are issued for tropical areas by the Tropical Prediction Center in Miami and the Central Pacific Hurricane Center in Honolulu. These advisories are issued at least four times a day when needed and extend out to 72 hours. Outside of the hurricane season, tropical weather discussions are also issued that are of use to sailors cruising tropical areas.

NWS Warnings

Small Craft Advisory—Winds 22–33 knots (sometimes for lower winds and bad sea state)

Gale Warning—Winds 34–47 knots

Storm Warning—Winds 47–64 knots

Hurricane Force Wind Warning—Winds in excess of 64 knots but not associated with a tropical cyclone (hurricane)

Tropical Storm Warning—Winds 34–63 knots associated with a tropical storm

Hurricane Warning—Winds in excess of 64 knots associated with a tropical cyclone (hurricane)

RECEIVING WEATHER DATA AND FORECASTS

Weather forecasts are of no use if sailors do not receive them. There are a number of ways by which sailors can receive forecasts at sea.

VHF-FM is often the most convenient means of receiving a forecast and most marine radios will have the main three WX channels (Channels 1–3) if not the full seven. Channels 4–7 are mainly used inland and by some stations on the Great Lakes. The broadcasts are on a continuous cycle and have a typical range of 25 nm; they will often include coastal observations from the local area. These are particularly useful to verify whether the forecast is progressing as expected and for timing features such as fronts and the development of sea breezes. Some receivers are automatically alarmed for severe weather warnings.

The Coast Guard also broadcasts on VHF Channel 22A after an initial call on 16, and for boats farther from land forecasts are transmitted on MF and HF radio frequencies. Navtex receivers are often found on blue-water yachts and will receive forecasts up to about 200nm offshore.

A great deal of information about the dissemination of the NWS marine forecasts can be found on the Marine and Coastal Weather Services Home Page.

Not many years ago, having a weather fax machine on board a yacht was considered the height of luxury, while the majority of us huddled by the radio listening to the forecast.

With modern communications and computers, we can turn a chart table into a mini NWS, producing forecasts neatly overlaid on navigational charts. The Internet has added a huge selection of additional information, while a dedicated antenna and black box will spew out satellite pictures from polar orbiting satellites to help clarify the situation.

The limitations are the speed of Internet access and the cost of connecting to it by mobile or satellite phone. Speeds are improving all the time although there can be a nasty shock when the bills for this technology arrive.

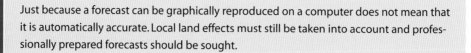

Just because a forecast can be graphically reproduced on a computer does not mean that it is automatically accurate. Local land effects must still be taken into account and professionally prepared forecasts should be sought.

FORECASTS FOR TRIP PLANNING

A lot of planning can be done ashore so we will look at what is available before going afloat and what we should be aiming for once sailing.

Any list of good weather sites will be out of date almost before it is published, but those given in the Appendix are ones that have been used and found reliable in the past. The information available on the Internet can be split into two categories: forecasts and observations. The forecasts are from various computer models and not only show surface pressure, but give wind arrows, temperatures, and other variables of varying usefulness.

The NOAA Marine Forecasts page is a good place to start and links from here will give us text forecasts for coastal, offshore, and high seas areas, along with any warnings.

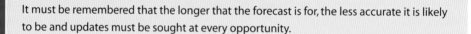

It must be remembered that the longer that the forecast is for, the less accurate it is likely to be and updates must be sought at every opportunity.

For any planning, synoptic charts are a must and the charts also found from the marine forecasts page show Pacific and Atlantic charts, both analysis and forecasts extending to 96 hours (see Weather Briefing Packages on page 141). The Caribbean and tropical waters are also covered along with general synoptic charts for the U.S. Most of these charts are also available through weather fax.

For longer term there are a number of sites that show weather charts for an extended forecast. The website of the U.S. Navy's Fleet Numerical Meteorology and Oceanography Center (https://www.fnmoc.navy.mil/PUBLIC/index.html) is useful and includes variables such as expected rainfall rates as well as over ocean wind speeds and wave heights. These charts extend to give a 180-hour forecast but because they are purely computer generated, they do not show fronts in the way we are used to seeing them. Rainfall rates give a good indication where these fronts are expected to be, enabling a good estimate to be made.

A word of caution—the wind arrows correspond to the synoptic chart from a particular model. The models will not always agree; therefore it is not a good idea to keep swapping between models.

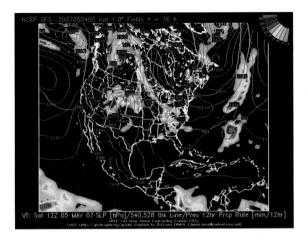

Surface pressure and rain from U.S. Navy's Fleet Numerical Meteorology and Oceanography Center. The passage of fronts can be seen from the rainfall. (Fleet Numerical Meteorology and Oceanography Center)

Forecast surface wind and wave heights. (Fleet Numerical Meteorology and Oceanography Center)

This satellite photo shows the weather and cloud cover for much of North America. (NASA Earth Science Office)

Meteorological observations are particularly useful as they are fact and not open to interpretation. The National Data Buoy Center has a huge network of data recording buoys that can be accessed via the Internet and also via a cell phone from on board. This is the closest we can get to real-time data about what is happening at sea. These reports cover the whole of the coastal U.S. and the Great Lakes as well as other parts of the world. There are also commercial providers of wind reports and local forecasts and when sailing in a new area a search on the Internet, or a chat to local sailors, will produce a list of the best sources.

Up-to-date analysis charts are also available on the web showing the station circles and the weather. These can be compared to the model charts to check how well the forecast is performing.

Satellite pictures add to the observations as they clearly show fronts and clouds. Cold fronts can be seen the most clearly with cumulus clouds behind. The analysis of satellite pictures on their own is difficult, but by comparing them to the synoptic charts it helps to bring the weather alive.

Rain radar is something that we have become used to from watching TV forecasts. It is very useful ashore when checking how quickly a front or system can pass through. Once away from Internet access, the information is quickly out of date; however, for larger boats with onboard radar, squalls and rain will show up clearly on a normal marine set. In the tropics, rainsqualls, and the likely strong winds that come with them, can be monitored successfully to get an idea if they will hit or miss.

Keep surfing, as each day new sites are springing up. After a while, you will decide on a small group of sites that you use regularly and stick to. They are all raw data with no, or very little, forecaster input and must be used with caution alongside dedicated marine forecasts.

FORECASTS ON BOARD

Weather fax is one of the most useful sources of forecasts when away from the land. It is received through an SSB radio, either as a stand-alone unit, or connected to a laptop computer. Most of its output consists of synoptic charts, sometimes with wind speeds or wave heights added. The fax transmission follows a schedule that can be found on the Internet (www.nws.noaa.gov/om/marine/rfax.pdf), which give schedules for around the world. Schedules can also be found in some almanacs and dedicated publications.

Synoptic charts are one of the few things that are standard throughout the world so these are particularly useful when long-distance cruising. Be aware though, some of the charts are transmitted for aviators so check that the one received is for sea level (MSLP). The upper-air charts can be useful; however a high level of meteorological training is necessary to get the best from them. They are generated from the same computer models as the surface charts; therefore any indications of changes in the upper atmosphere should be picked up by the surface charts giving continuity between them. (See below for more on the topic of upper-air charts.)

One of the most exciting developments is that meteorological data can now be downloaded from the Internet or received via e-mail, and overlaid onto an electronic navigational chart. Some software will animate a series of forecasts covering several days, to help visualize the changing weather pattern in this navigational context. Grib files, used by soft-

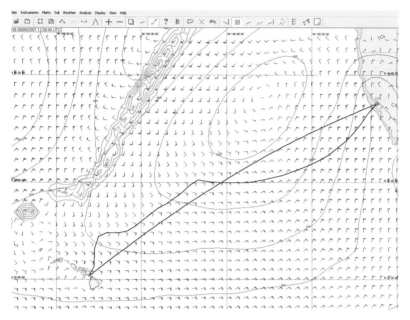

Wind arrows, surface pressure, and an optimum route. The green contours are rainfall which gives a good indication to the position of fronts. (Expedition Software)

ware such as MaxSea, Expedition, and Raytech, are produced free of charge by NOAA and some commercial providers. Many meteorological variables can be received in this way; for sailors the wind speed and direction are of obvious interest, as well as surface pressure, expected rainfall, and sea state.

The files you get are part of a computer-generated forecast that covers the whole world, with a resolution of about 50km. The resolution is gradually getting better, but at present, there is a risk that small-scale features will be missed. Some Grib providers offer a higher resolution for small geographical areas; these usually attract a subscription charge.

The absence of fronts drawn onto the chart is strange at first, although their positions can be estimated from the kinks in the isobars and/or the abrupt change in wind direction. Some Grib files include rainfall rates, which help pinpoint the position of fronts. Sailing through a front is likely to give a more abrupt wind change than the computer predicts.

The ability to enter the boat's sailing characteristics (polars), and to use a routing program that combines the weather forecast with the polars to produce an optimum course, is a very powerful routing tool. How many of us have sat at the chart table wondering if it would be better to tack now or later? Or how much to bear off and where we will be when the expected wind swing arrives?

Check Against Reality

Whichever model you use, checking to see how it compares with reality is all-important. Whatever the computer may say, it is the weather that is real, and once the model has strayed from reality it is unlikely to find its way back. It may be low tech, but the barometer is still one of the most important tools for the navigator. Combined with wind direction and strength it will tell you where you are within a system and gives an idea on how close to reality the model is.

There are other limitations too, particularly close to land where local conditions will modify the wind fields considerably.

Technology is continually changing and for a small cost personal graphical forecasts can be e-mailed directly to a boat at sea or to the crew ashore for planning before the start of a passage. The Internet has many sites offering forecasts for planning up to ten days in advance as well as the opportunity to buy dedicated forecasts. All will need some user input and will, to some extent, need to be modified for local land effects. Mobile phones can also receive forecasts for specific areas.

MORE ON TYPES OF CHARTS AND FORECASTING DATA

UPPER-AIR CHARTS

Throughout the book we have concentrated on surface weather charts. For the majority of us, this is all we will ever look at—if we have a series of forecast surface charts from the NWS, we are unlikely to be able to improve on them.

However, when sailing long distances we are not always fortunate in receiving these surface charts. We may have to rely on upper-air charts to help understand what is happening at the surface, and to help us to make our own forecasts.

When computer models generate a forecast they split the atmosphere into many layers, which are based on air pressure, not altitude. Charts are produced for several of these layers, and they are labeled with a mb height, usually in the series 850mb, 750mb, 500mb, and 300mb. The different heights show different features. For example, the 850mb and 750mb heights help to position precipitation and fronts, and 300mb charts show the position of the jet stream. Although charts of different heights can be found on the Internet, it is the 500mb chart that is regularly published and is readily available. This is because the 500mb charts are of use when forecasting where systems may develop and move. They also show where the bottom of the jet stream is, as indicated by increased wind speeds shown on the chart.

Internationally it has been agreed that standard surface pressure is 1013.2mb, which gives the average altitudes for the different pressures as shown on the accompanying table.

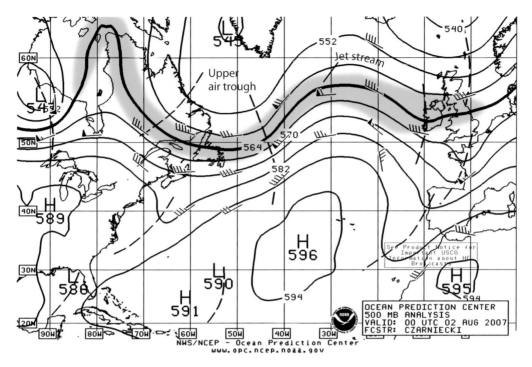

A 500mb chart for the Atlantic Ocean showing the jet stream and a number of upper air troughs. (National Weather Service)

The spinning earth forms long, horizontal waves in the upper atmosphere in an unbroken series extending around the world, with troughs heading south and ridges to the north. These long waves, called Rossby waves, mark boundaries between warm and cold air masses. Thus, a trough shows where cold air is moving south in the upper atmosphere, and a ridge shows where warm air is moving north. On 500mb charts, lows are likely to form under the troughs and highs in the ridges.

The curves of equal altitude on the upper-air charts are spaced at intervals of tens of meters and denote the local altitude at which the pressure of 500mb will be found. The 500mb altitude is lower in cold, dense air than in warmer air, so we can expect to find

Standard Pressures and Their Average Altitudes

Standard Pressure (mb)	Altitude	
	Feet	Meters
1013.2	0	0
850	4781	1457
750	8091	2466
500	18289	5574
300	30065	9164

lower values to the north and higher altitudes to the south. Certain altitudes are indicative of specific conditions; for example, you can generally avoid strong surface winds by staying south of where the 500mb height is at 5640 meters (labeled 564 on the maps), while the 528 curve will give a good proximity to the edge of a snowfall band.

Troughs in upper-air charts, as on surface charts, are marked by dashed lines. Upper-air troughs are likely to have areas of surface development beneath them. The 500mb chart also indicates the position of the jet stream, either with wind arrows or isotachs (lines of equal wind speed). When wind speeds over 100 knots are combined with a trough, rapid development of a surface low is possible.

There is, however, an internal consistency within the computer model that generates the charts for different pressure levels. Thus, if we can see an area of likely development by using the 500mb chart, it will be reflected in the surface chart of the same time. One might therefore conclude that a 500mb chart is never necessary, but life is not perfect. If your shipboard weather fax receiver is susceptible to interference, the 500mb chart may be all you can access. Then too, you can use a 500mb chart to judge whether a surface forecast is likely to under- or overestimate wind speeds.

Some sailors swear by the 500mb charts, while others rely exclusively on surface charts. Here are some rules of thumb that sailors use with upper-air charts:

- By staying south of the 564 line we can generally avoid winds of greater than Force 6 in the summer (22–27 knots) and Force 7 in the winter (28–33 knots). This is a generalization that excludes local effects and is largely based on anecdotal evidence. The 564 line is shown as bold on NWS charts but not always on charts from other sources.
- Lows are likely to be steered by the winds at the 500mb or jet stream level. This can be useful when estimating future storm tracks beyond the normal surface forecast time period.
- As mentioned, upper-air troughs are areas of development and, if combined with a locally strong jet stream, will generate rapid storm development at the surface. If we already have a low shown on the surface charts and we see another trough approaching in the upper airflow, then we have the potential for a rapidly deepening system and a significant increase in wind.

Historically, rapid development of a low has been termed a "bomb," although meteorologists are more likely to describe it nowadays as explosive or rapid cyclogenesis. This is most likely to happen in the fall and winter months, when a big influx of cold air from the north meets warm moist air from the south. This implies a deep upper-air trough moving the cold air south. Warm ocean currents—the Gulf Stream, for example—add power in the form of heat, and rapid development can follow. Bombs tend to deepen rapidly for 24 hours, then deepen at a slower rate for an additional 12 hours. Little further deepening occurs after 36 hours. Any pressure drop in a storm of 18mb or more over 24 hours may be termed a bomb or explosive cyclogenesis.

Bombs are most likely over the ocean, particularly where there is warm water to serve as a heat and moisture source for overlying air, although they have been known to happen over the land as well.

OBSERVATIONS

Up-to-date observations help to verify forecasts, help in timing fronts, and can give advance warning of what is on its way. Supplementing forecasts, observations give a sense of reality to a forecast but it must be remembered that shore stations (particularly airports, where many of the observations originate) are subject to land effects so they may not give an accurate representation of the overall picture. Buoy reports, however, give a more representative report for an area.

Close to land, listening to the radio and getting the local forecast is still necessary as this will give a professionally prepared forecast using models with a much higher resolution, as well as a greater array of observations to give an accurate local picture. Each bit of information is just another piece in the puzzle and just as no one should rely on one navigation system, neither should you rely on one piece of weather information.

SATELLITE PICTURES

We see them every night on television being used to explain where bands of rain and cloud are likely to be. On board, they are slow to download unless a dedicated receiver and aerial are used. Polar orbiting satellites give the best resolution but are only updated a few

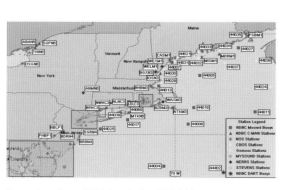

Buoy data from NOAA website. (NOAA)

Satellite picture of the Pacific with weather chart overlay. (Naval Research Laboratory, Monterey)

times a day; geostationary satellites are positioned over the equator and are updated regularly. Because of the earth's curvature, geostationary satellite pictures become hard to interpret in high latitudes but are very good in the tropics.

Visible images are at a better resolution than infrared but are obviously limited to daylight hours. The infrared measures the temperatures of the top of the clouds: the whiter the color the colder the cloud top.

It's particularly useful to compare the satellite pictures with the synoptic charts. A site that does this for us is the Monterey Naval Research Laboratory. Here we can see a composite picture, made from different satellite pictures, with sea level pressure overlaid, or alternatively with expected wind strength in the form of wind arrows.

SYNTHESIZE DATA FROM ALL SOURCES

With all the information available, we can, and should be able to, improve on the forecast in the short term, and for the relatively small area that we sail in.

THE ORDER OF INTERPRETING WEATHER DATA

Weather data should be interpreted in the following order:

- Study synoptic charts to get general conditions.
- Compare barometer, wind speed and direction, and clouds with those expected from the synoptic chart. Verify the forecast.

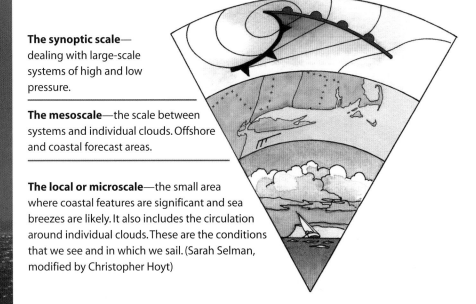

The synoptic scale—dealing with large-scale systems of high and low pressure.

The mesoscale—the scale between systems and individual clouds. Offshore and coastal forecast areas.

The local or microscale—the small area where coastal features are significant and sea breezes are likely. It also includes the circulation around individual clouds. These are the conditions that we see and in which we sail. (Sarah Selman, modified by Christopher Hoyt)

- Use the forecast general synopsis to see how features will move and the area forecasts to give the average wind for your sea area.
- Use the coastal waters forecast to see how the professionals think the general landmass will affect the wind.
- Refine the forecasts for your position within the sea areas for the movement of the synoptic systems.
- Look at the land and modify the forecast for land effects, both mechanical and thermal. Land forecasts from commercial radio will often give an expected maximum high temperature.
- Is a sea breeze likely?
- Are there any weather dangers—squalls, thunderstorms, fog, etc? Keep a good weather eye, as there are always signs.
- Watch the clouds for local circulation.
- Check tides to avoid wind against tide conditions, especially around headlands or where the tidal streams or currents are strong.
- Continually monitor and log the wind, barometer, and clouds, and compare them with the forecast.

By continually following the above you should be able to stay one step ahead of the weather, and by doing so have a safer and more enjoyable voyage.

PLAN, OBSERVE, GO!

Wherever and whenever we go boating—whether we're going for an evening cruise in local waters, making an offshore passage to or from the Caribbean, or racing around the world—we need to make some form of a plan.

We are all aware of the weather—all the time, even in our workaday life. Although our commute may be from the garage at home to an underground parking lot at work, the weather affects road conditions and can extend the duration and the safety of the journey. We plan for all this informally; when it rains, for example, we leave home a few minutes earlier or expect to arrive a few minutes late.

When we are sailing, however, the impacts of weather are more immediate, and if we do not plan for and take note of deteriorating weather, we can get into difficulties. In advance of any sailing, therefore, we watch how the weather is developing and get a feel for the systems that may be coming or going. We gather weather forecasts from the television or online and supplement these by looking out the window.

AN INSHORE SAIL

Let's see how the weather-information-gathering process might work for an afternoon sail on Puget Sound. A good place to start would be the synoptic charts. The charts from the National Weather Service (NWS) for the Pacific (see page 50) give us an indication of what to expect over the next few days. From these, we get a general pattern of what is going on, which helps us decide whether or not to go sailing at all. A deep low barreling in from the Pacific may make us think again, or change the timing of our plans.

We will also look at the coastal waters forecast for the area. This splits the days and nights for the following 4–5 days, giving wind directions and speeds as well as expected wave heights. Finally we will monitor the local weather radio station for a local forecast and reports. Almost all the coastal waters of North America, including the Great Lakes are covered and often two areas will overlap. To avoid interference these are on different frequencies usually on channels WX-1, 2, or 3 on the marine radio.

So now we have a very good idea of what to expect. We will still need to use our experience and knowledge to estimate where the wind will accelerate between islands and along sounds, where we are likely to get stronger winds and where shelter will be found. It is also worth watching the clouds; hills may trigger showers and squalls which when we look at satellite or radar pictures are usually not evenly distributed, but are in lanes downwind of a land feature such as a headland or hill. Where mountains come close to the sea we may get katabatic winds blowing down the slopes, which at night can make uncomfortable anchorages. These can be particularly nasty in the spring with snow-covered mountains near the coast.

Using our experience and knowledge we can therefore estimate how the land is likely to affect the wind and where the best places to sail are for the given general conditions.

GOING OFFSHORE

Ocean passages are more of a challenge in getting the weather right and also enjoying the passage. Most problems, but not all, occur when we are sailing out of season—but getting the season right is not always as straightforward as it sounds.

Take, for instance, a voyage from the Caribbean to Newport, Rhode Island, a voyage undertaken by many yachts each year. We want to leave before the start of hurricane season but the farther north we get in spring and early summer the greater the risk of a gale.

Many yachts leave in May after Antigua Race Week, but before the official start of the hurricane season in June. We do, however, get some storm formation ahead of the official season. In 2007, subtropical storm warnings were issued by the National Hurricane Center in early May for Andrea, the first named storm of the year.

For a voyage of this length we start by studying the Pilot charts (called Routing charts in the UK). These can be bought at chart agents around the world and most (soon to be all) of the Pilot charts can be downloaded from the Internet.

These charts split the ocean up into 5° squares (2° in places), and show wind roses for each square based on many years of historical data. Each wind rose shows the percentage of time the wind blows from each direction and its average strength during each month. On the charts are also indications of currents, chance of gales, average pressure, likelihood of fog, wave heights, and tracks of tropical and subtropical storms.

Pilot charts provide a huge amount of information to help plan a route giving favorable winds and avoiding storms. It must be stressed, however, that these are averages and adverse weather is still a possibility.

Having planned a route using the Pilot charts, we then look at the long-range forecast from the synoptic and forecast charts. A small change of heading may keep us one side of a front or the other depending on the expected wind direction. The weather charts will also indicate where systems will track and the strength of the wind likely to be found. We will

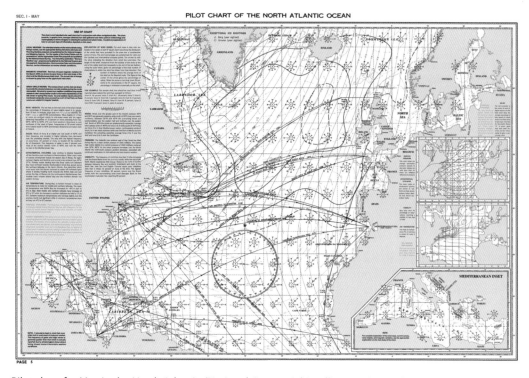

Pilot chart for May in the North Atlantic. (National Geospatial-Intelligence Agency)

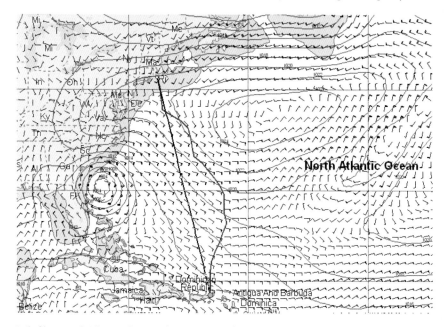

Grib files overlaid on a chart with a suggested optimum route. (Expedition Software)

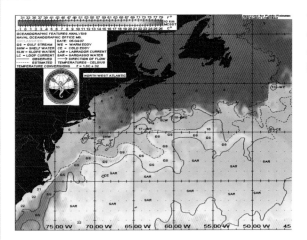

The northern part of the Gulf Stream. Choosing where and when to cross the current is important. (Naval Oceanographic Service)

also listen to, or look at, forecasts for the local area. Taking into account sea breezes and where winds might accelerate as they are funneled around the islands will make the difference between going out into the full force of the wind or having a couple of hours motoring to charge the batteries and make sure all is well.

Many yachts will now use Grib files to help plan their route. Grib files are a standard way of transmitting large amounts of meteorological data. For sailors, the wind speed and direction as well as surface pressure are of great concern. As the files do not show weather fronts, rainfall rates can also usually be shown via Grib forecasts.

Grib files can be overlaid on most electronic navigation charts (depending on your software) and on many it is possible to use a weather routing function that matches the weather to your boat's performance and will give you an optimum route. This software will also put in tides and ocean currents and include these in the computation of the route. This, however, only gives an indication as the input from the weather files and the boat's performance data are never 100 percent accurate. Ocean racers spend huge amounts of time "tweaking" the Grib files and perfecting the boat's performance polars.

A voyage of 1500 or so miles from the Caribbean to Newport is going to take a variable amount of time depending on the size of the boat and the weather. Along the way we need to be able to pick up weather forecasts and have the flexibility to change our plans if necessary. Most yachts will have a plan to call in at Bermuda if inclement weather is forecast, or just for a break, a run ashore, and to pick up the latest weather information. With lows and cold fronts coming off the North American Coast, Bermuda can become quite busy as yachts wait for a change in conditions. The Bermudan Weather Service gives good marine forecasts and charts.

While at sea receiving information can be difficult. Weather fax and/or the high seas forecast by HF radio is still one of the most reliable means; however many yachts have e-mail access via satellite phone. Grib files and synoptic charts can be received via e-mail. Communication costs can be high. Full Internet access is still prohibitively expensive, but getting cheaper and faster every year.

Active cold fronts along with lows are the most likely to give us strong wind along the route but we must be aware that tropical storms may move north into the subtropics. Also of importance is the Gulf Stream; this river of warm water brings much heat energy north and lows may intensify over the warm water bringing stronger than forecast winds. Crossing the Gulf Stream with the wind against the current is at best uncomfortable and can be extremely dangerous, as the seas quickly steepen and break. This is not just a small tidal race but can be of boat-breaking severity and must not be underestimated.

As we approach the coast additional radio forecasts can be received which, along with the weather charts, should ensure no unpleasant surprises.

A comprehensive weather briefing package, providing forecasts for several days, can be downloaded from the National Weather Service. See Weather Briefing on page 141.

A QUICK SAIL

Our final example is for a local evening race:

For an evening race around the buoys at the local yacht club, we may think that getting weather forecasts is not worth the effort. The race will last for an hour or so and we get what we get. To some extent this is true, but a weather forecast will indicate anything over the horizon. Thunderstorms or tornadoes may have been triggered by the heat of the day and could be just minutes away.

A greater knowledge of the weather will give an advantage when racing. Identifying what is a sea breeze and where it will die first will help in understanding what happens next. Realizing that it is a sea breeze at all, and therefore likely to be in decline through the evening, helps in selecting the correct sail for the race. If, however, it is a building wind from an approaching low, our tactics and sail plan are likely to be different.

I can think of no time when I would go sailing without getting a weather forecast before leaving the dock. For a short race I may rely on the local weather radio forecast; however the longer the sail the more time I spend planning.

The more successful the racing skipper, the greater his/her knowledge and the better his/her preparation before any race, be it a "fun" race or the America's Cup.

The start of a Thursday evening J/24 race off Camden, Maine. (International Marine/McGraw-Hill)

13

Sailing Areas of North America

The U.S. extends from the arctic to the tropics if we include the Virgin Islands and Hawaii. Over such a large area as this, the weather is very different from the north to the south and from East Coast to West Coast. Sailing on inland waters has its own set of special circumstances. And we can even extend our sailing season—iceboating has been going on for over 100 years!

The majority of our sailing, however, is done in the disturbed pattern of the mid-latitude lows. Weather systems come from the west in a series of lows broken by periods of high pressure. The jet stream that steers the lows moves north in the summer and farther south in the winter helping to give us four definite seasons of the year. Coastal waters keep the temperatures milder along the coast than inland. Large-scale icing of the waters is restricted to the center of the continent around the Great Lakes.

Because the weather can be so different in the various sailing areas I have included a short description of the weather likely to be found around the U.S. It is not a comprehensive list but typical of the conditions likely to be found.

THE PACIFIC COAST

The Pacific coast is dominated by the semipermanent Pacific High pressure system. This high moves north and south with the seasons, intensifying as it moves north in the summer. The high pressure blocks the transient lows from the west forcing them to track farther north in the summer and south in the winter. This results in stormier, more unsettled weather the farther north we are, and more settled weather to the south.

Along the coast, the cold California current flows southward and this colder water helps to generate the fogs that we associate with this coast. This fog is advection fog (see Chapter 10), created as the warm moist air from the Pacific crosses the cooler coastal waters. This relatively shallow layer of air will often be referred to as the *marine layer*; where wind, temperature, and visibility is strongly influenced by the ocean. This is the boundary layer (see page 11). Over the water the air takes on some of the ocean's characteristics, namely moisture and temperature—this can be quite different from the boundary layer found over land which will be considerably drier and warmer during the day, colder at night. Due to

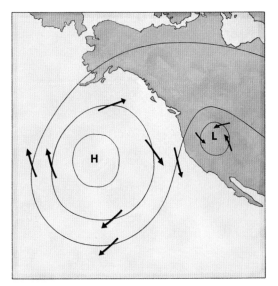

Typical summer weather pattern on the West Coast. The Pacific High has moved north and a thermal low has developed over Southern California. (Christopher Hoyt)

the cool seawater temperature, an inversion—where the air temperature increases with height—often occurs. Coastal upwelling also occurs where, after steady northerly winds from the high pressure, surface water is moved away and is replaced by colder water from greater depths.

ALASKA AND THE PACIFIC NORTHWEST

Starting from the the north and moving southward, the weather on the Pacific coast overall is dominated by the relative positions of the Pacific High and the *Aleutian Low*. Rather than a static low-pressure system, it is more of a succession of lows crossing the Pacific. Taking an average pressure shows an area of low pressure centered near the Aleutian Islands. The prevailing westerly winds are warm and moist causing clouds and rainfall on the coastal hills and mountains. The climate can best be described as maritime, keeping winters mild and summers cool with a high rainfall.

Synoptic charts will show lows becoming less frequent in the summer with an increase in storms through the autumn and winter. Keep in mind that there are a number of definitions for winter—astronomically it is between the winter solstice on December 21 (or thereabouts) and the March equinox; however meteorologists and farmers usually refer to winter as the three coldest months of December, January, and February.

During the summer months, winds are predominantly west or southwest and the chance of gales diminishes. Lows will pass close to the Aleutian Islands. From South Alaska to Seattle the coast is fringed with islands; while this gives some sheltered cruising grounds, the land forces moist air aloft. This produces clouds and rain where there is clear sky out to sea. Lows that form and build out in the oceans are most likely to look like the textbook lows, with warm fronts and sectors ahead of the cold front.

THE NORTHERN CALIFORNIAN COAST

During the summer the Pacific High pushes most of the lows and their associated fronts to the north. Summer months therefore have a mainly west or northwest flow. The thermal (heat) low to the southeast reinforces the wind giving a strong sea breeze during the afternoons, reaching 20 knots or more (see Sea Breezes on page 62–67). With the breeze driven by the general pressure gradient, the afternoon wind can stay late into the evening—sometimes until after midnight—before dying away completely. There will also be considerable differences in different parts of San Francisco Bay, the main sailing area along the coast.

As the breeze crosses the cooler inshore waters, advection fog can form. This gives us the stunning photos of the top of the Golden Gate Bridge visible while below is obscured; but this makes sailing difficult. The fog can lift with a strong day breeze forming stratus clouds.

During the winter the Pacific High tends to drift south and the Pacific storms also tend to track farther south. Frontal weather will become the norm with settled high pressure in between. High pressure can bring radiation fog over the land that struggles to clear through the winter's day persisting until the high pressure moves away—this is sometimes termed "anticyclonic gloom" and is made worse by pollution and smog.

THE SOUTHERN CALIFORNIA COAST

The coast changes direction and character south of Point Arguello and Point Conception; there is often also a change in the weather at this point. From here to Mexico the climate is subtropical with light west to northwest winds through the summer. The Pacific High pressure dominates the weather farther north and few fronts penetrate the high this far south during the summer months. Low pressure over the deserts (thermal low) helps to generate daily sea breezes maintaining comfortable temperatures ashore. The geography and climate means that there is often a temperature inversion over the coastal area that traps any pollution in the lowest layers of the atmosphere (the marine layer) causing the infamous Southern California smog.

Poor visibility is a feature of the coastal waters, more in terms of smog, fog, and low stratus trapped in the marine layer below approximately 1000 feet (300m) than the advection fog of farther north. Advection fog is still possible but it is not as widespread or as frequent as farther north.

A number of times each year the normal pattern of northwesterly winds is interrupted with more southerly coastal winds. There is an increase in the thickness of the marine layer and an increase in stratus clouds. This is known as the *Catalina Eddy* as it is associated with a cyclonic or counterclockwise circulation in the surface winds with the center near Santa Catalina Island. The southerly wind extends to about 60 miles from the coast. Although there is greater cloud cover, visibility will often improve as there is greater mixing of the marine layer; the temperature may drop as much as 13°F (7°C). Because the Catalina Eddy is relatively small—maybe only 120 miles across—it is not picked up well on global models. There will be a stronger than usual northerly wind flow near Point Arguello and some lee troughing (see page 23) from the San Rafael mountains becomes evident. In addition an extension of the heat low northward helps develop the circulation. Where we are in relation to the eddy will determine the wind direction we will experience and can turn a seemingly sheltered anchorage into a nasty surprise.

Leaving Santa Barbara Harbor. (Helen Tibbs)

During the winter months Pacific lows can affect the area but to a generally less extent than farther north. Although hurricanes pass well to the west they can bring heavy rain to Southern California. A strong ENSO event (see Chapter 15) is also likely to bring increased rainfall to the area. The Santa Ana wind is another local wind that can cause problems and is discussed on page 58.

THE EAST COAST

Ranging from the Canadian Maritimes to Florida, weather conditions can be very different along the East Coast. The majority of the coast is influenced by disturbed westerly winds and the polar front. The position of the jet stream is often shown on the nightly TV weather forecasts due to its influence on lows and their tracks. During the winter months the lows or storm tracks move to the south and retreat northward again in the spring and summer. This gives us the variable wind and weather associated with the lows. In addition, the whole of the coast is at risk of hurricane strikes that have moved north from the Caribbean, although the farther north we are the lower the chance of a direct hit. As a hurricane passes over cooler water some of its source of energy is cut off and the characteristics change; a hurricane will sometimes combine with a mid-latitude low.

In addition to the lows from the west, the Bermuda High to the east also plays its part. As the jet stream moves north in the spring and early summer, the Bermuda High (sometimes referred to as the *Azores High*) becomes more established, bringing more settled weather to the coast.

The warm waters of the Gulf Stream and the cold Labrador Current also play their part in influencing the weather.

THE GULF STREAM

The Gulf Stream is a warm water current flowing northward through the Straits of Florida following the coast to the vicinity of Cape Hatteras where it swings away from the coast and meanders east to northeast across the Atlantic. (See Chapter 12.) It eventually reaches Europe where it is called the North Atlantic Drift, with one branch pushing northeast to Norway and the other heading south to become part of the Canary Current. The Gulf Stream is an example of a western boundary current found on the west side of oceans and is important in

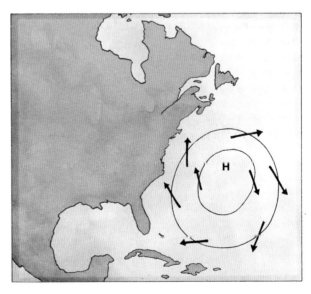

Typical summer weather pattern on the East Coast. The Bermuda High brings warm moist air to the coastal regions. (Christopher Hoyt)

helping to regulate the temperature of the planet, moving vast amounts of heat away from the equator. It is estimated that about 40 percent of the heat transport in the Northern Hemisphere comes from ocean currents.

The Gulf Stream also has a significant effect on the climate of America, bringing a great source of heat energy along the East Coast. It is the warm moist air associated with the Gulf Stream that creates the fog over the Grand Banks as it meets the cold Arctic water heading south.

With so much heat energy it is not surprising that lows will form on and deepen near the Gulf Stream. The northern edge of the stream is called the North Wall and will often have much stronger wind than elsewhere. The North Wall is sometimes marked by huge convective clouds (cumulus and cumulonimbus). The warm waters of the Gulf Stream can cause hurricanes to intensify and are also partly responsible for the humid conditions found in the summer in the southern East Coast states.

If the wind is against the current the sea conditions quickly become dangerous with large breaking seas; however, if the wind and the current act together great distances can be covered. The analysis and the use of eddies in the current go a long way to winning the hotly contested biennial Newport to Bermuda race.

Having crossed the Gulf Stream a number of times, I can attest that conditions can be very varied from horrendous wave conditions in only a moderate northerly wind, to flat calm without a ripple on the water. It is an area where the forecast should be closely monitored and avoided if there are any predictions for adverse weather crossing the current. The Gulf Stream has, however, produced record-breaking distances sailed in 24 hours during ocean yacht races.

CANADIAN MARITIMES

The Canadian Maritime includes the northern area of the Atlantic Coast, Nova Scotia, and southern Newfoundland. The area is close to the tracks of lows that cross North America and it is also close to lows that form or deepen near the East Coast. So at all times of the year we are close to storm tracks bringing rapidly changing conditions. These lows (storms) are less severe in the summer than the winter, but still bring very changeable weather. On average one named Caribbean tropical storm passes within 300 miles of Newfoundland each year. The cold Labrador Current flowing from the northeast keeps temperatures low throughout the summer and icebergs drifting south with the current are closely monitored.

THE NORTHEAST

Firmly in the band of easterly moving lows, the northeast coast of the U.S. can have very variable weather. During the summer months, southwesterly winds are most common. However, we can have winds from any direction. The Labrador Current brings cold water south to the area and the cooling effect of the cold water brings many fogs. Fogs in Maine form at sea over the cold-water inshore currents and on some days there may be fog offshore while bays and harbors with warmer water are fog free. Sea breezes can develop, sometimes bringing fog inshore with them.

Lows can track north or south of the area and the most violent storms are from the northeast and are referred to as nor'easters. In the winter and spring (and occasionally

The Tax Day storm of April 2007. (NASA Earth Science Office)

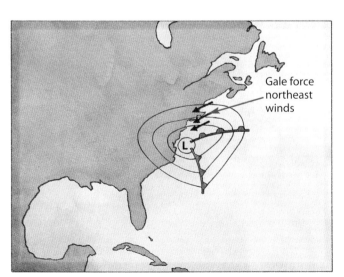

Gale force northeast winds

A typical nor'easter. A deep winter low passing farther south than usual will generate strong northeasterly winds affecting the mid-Atlantic region and states farther north. These lows can bring storm- or hurricane-force winds and can cause extensive damage. (Christopher Hoyt)

the fall), deep depressions pass to the south, putting the northeast coast in the upper left quadrant of the storms. This brings strong NE winds to the coast often accompanied by heavy rain. Some of the storms cause a great deal of disruption and are named by the media, such as the Tax Day storm of April 2007.

The farther south on the east coast, the greater the effect of the Bermuda High and also the greater the effect of the Gulf Stream.

THE MID-ATLANTIC STATES

The farther south we move, the more the Bermuda High dominates the summer weather. Except in midwinter, lows mainly pass to the north of the mid-Atlantic coast. The geography of the land plays its part with the Appalachian Mountains tending to deflect the depressions north. During the summer months a warm airflow from the Bermuda High picks up moisture crossing the Gulf Stream, bringing hot humid conditions. The Chesapeake Bay is noted for light winds and fine weather with a daily sea breeze. There can, however, be thunderstorms and strong squalls along the coast.

FLORIDA AND THE GULF OF MEXICO

Subtropical sailing with mainly light winds is the norm for this area of the U.S. During the winter months, cold fronts may sweep down from the north bringing colder northerly winds while the summer is mild with predominantly warm moist wind. Thunderstorms are common through the summer and there is always the threat of hurricanes making landfall on the coast.

THE GREAT LAKES

Although called lakes, the large Great Lakes are like small inland seas producing their own microclimates and regular sea breezes, or, more accurately, lake breezes. The area is well covered by marine forecasts from both the U.S. and Canada, with the Canadian forecasts being mainly in metric units.

The position of these lakes in the center of the continent does not create the temperature moderation effect brought on by the sea that is usual around the coast. These colder temperatures allow ice to form and sailing is curtailed for the winter months. These months also have stormy conditions as lows cross the country. Some of these lows originate in the Pacific, intensify over Canada, and are named Alberta Lows.

The weather here is variable and can change quickly. Looking at weather charts, there always seems to be something happening over the Great Lakes—cold dry air from the north may be pushing in to mix with warm moist air from the south helping to develop or deepen lows. When sailing on the East Coast it is always worth watching what is happening at the Great Lakes as it gives advance warning of the weather to come.

During the summer months, lake breezes develop and thunderstorms are common along with the occasional waterspouts or tornadoes. Ocean sailors sometimes dismiss the Great Lakes, but anyone who has sailed in the Chicago to Mackinac race recognizes it as a classic and knows better than to underestimate the weather here.

INLAND SAILING

Each weekend a large number of boaters head for lakes and rivers for a variety of water-sports. While the sea has its own set of challenges for sailors, lakes and rivers present a new set of challenges and dangers.

We saw earlier that the surface wind is slower over the land than the sea due to the effect of friction (drag); this will also have the effect of backing the wind to a greater extent over land than over the sea. If the land were flat, this would result in the wind being around 20–40° backed from the direction of the isobars from our surface charts. However, as the wind will follow the path of least resistance, it closely follows the topography of the land and will funnel down valleys, which may be at a very different direction from the gradient or synoptic wind. Wind strengths may, in theory, be only about half that of at sea for the same pressure gradient, but large differences in wind strength may be found just a few miles apart. Over large lakes we find that the wind increases over the water due to less friction; therefore we can expect a stronger wind on the downwind side of a lake than the upwind. A

Over large lakes the wind tends to accelerate and veer a few degrees (unless the lake is very cold). (Christopher Hoyt)

Over large lakes as the air reaches the lee shore there will be some convergence (C) and ascent of air. This will cause clouds to form at the lee end of the lake. D is an area of divergence as the air accelerates. (Christopher Hoyt)

very cold lake however would cool and stabilize the air negating any increase. We may also find that there is a cloud buildup at the downwind end of the lake due to convergence.

These effects can be grouped together as mechanical or orographic (mountain-related) changes to the wind. We can add to this the "Chinook"—a warm, dry, often-violent wind found on the east side of the Rockies.

Winds in mountainous areas may have a daily pattern similar to the sea breezes of the oceans. These winds are usually described as valley and mountain winds or up- and down-slope winds. These can be so regular that a morning sail with a following wind to the end of the lake can be followed by a leisurely lunch. After lunch the afternoon valley wind will return us to our starting point, again sailing under spinnaker!

There is a great deal of similarity to the sea breeze circulation of the oceans and the mountain winds. The mountains heat during the day causing an upslope wind similar to the sea breeze. Like a sea breeze the existence of the upslope wind is indicated by cumulus clouds building over the mountaintops. Loved by glider pilots, these upslope, or anabatic, winds will also give a light afternoon breeze in lakes along the valley floor.

Nighttime cooling of the mountains reverses the flow and cold air drains down the valley often at a stronger force than the afternoon valley wind. These are downslope, or katabatic, winds. (See also Chapter 8.)

> **Katabatic wind**—a drainage or mountain wind also known as a downslope wind. Cold air.
> **Anabatic wind**—a wind that blows up a slope, heated by sunshine.

On large lakes we will get an afternoon lake breeze, which is the equivalent of a sea breeze. The different shores will behave differently depending on the direction of the gradient wind, with many localized effects, as few lakes are perfectly round and set on a flat plain. Hills and mountains will have a significant affect. The bigger the lake the closer the wind will follow the pattern that we would expect when sailing near the coast at sea. It is worth checking water temperatures as lakes may be fed by cold meltwater from the mountains and be considerably colder than expected. Not only will this give more mist and fog over the water, but can be a life-threatening danger should you fall in.

TREES AND OTHER BARRIERS TO THE WIND

Research has shown that a "medium-density" barrier, such as trees, vegetation, and other yachts will extend a wind shadow for many times the height of the object downwind. This has a significant effect to lake and river sailors whose course is often near the shoreline, and the wind is always offshore at some part of the lake.

Different barriers will have different effects. However, as a guide, trees and other medium-density barriers will affect the wind for something like 30 times the height of the object. Interestingly a solid barrier will have less of an effect than, for example, trees, in terms of the distance that it disturbs the wind, although the initial drop in wind will be greater. There have been a number of times when racing that I have cut the corner and got too close to the land only to watch my competitors take the longer route and sail around me.

FORECASTS

With the exception of the Great Lakes and a few rivers, our inland lakes and rivers do not have the marine weather forecast coverage of the coastal waters. The VHF-FM continual forecasts are not available and we have to rely upon local commercial radio, the TV, and Internet. While the average wind speed over inland waters is usually less than that over the sea, we must still take into account the passage of fronts, squalls, and thunderstorms, as well as local effects. On rivers, the speed of the current can quickly increase driven by rainfall many miles away. Beating against a strong current and headwinds makes progress slow or even impossible.

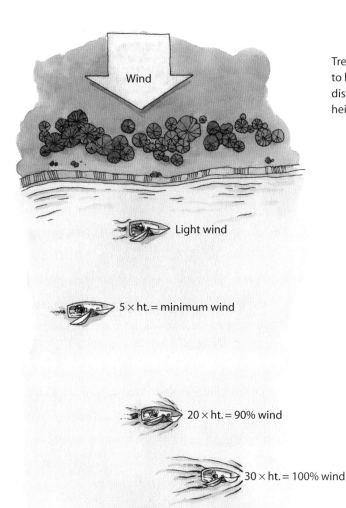

Trees and similar partial barriers tend to have an effect on wind strength to a distance of about 30 times their height. (Christopher Hoyt)

CHAPTER 14

Around the World

No book can cover all the possible weather patterns around the world, but we can look at the more famous (or infamous) winds likely to be met on an extended cruise.

TRADE WINDS AND TROPICAL SAILING

Every year, fortunate sailors are able to head to the Caribbean or Pacific in search of sailing among the islands of the trade wind belt.

The *trade winds* are steady winds found in both hemispheres on the eastern and equator sides of the subtropical high-pressure areas. They vary in position and strength year to year but rarely fail completely. Moderate steady wind and sunshine have made sailing in the trades almost legendary. With a full moon and spinnaker set, there can be few places that offer better sailing conditions.

Details of the extent and strength of trade winds can be found on Pilot or Routing charts.

As we sail westward in the trade winds there is an increase of moisture in the air, giving rise to more squally weather. These squalls range from a few cooling drops of rain to a tropical downpour with gale force gusts of wind. As a rule, a squall that is fast moving, with clouds of great vertical height, and rain, will give a strong gust on its leading edge. The circulation is similar to that of a thunderstorm, as described in Chapter 10.

This has led to a description of clouds as being "sucking" or "blowing." A cloud or squall that is developing will have a flow of air into the cloud, and when underneath it we will experience a lull in the wind. Once the rain starts to fall the cloud is said to be blowing and as it approaches we will experience a strong, sometimes gale force, gust of wind along with the rain.

The squalls are driven by the direction of the wind at a few thousand feet. This direction will usually be different from the surface wind. Typically (in the Northern Hemisphere) the direction of the squall will be from the right of the surface wind, as the surface wind

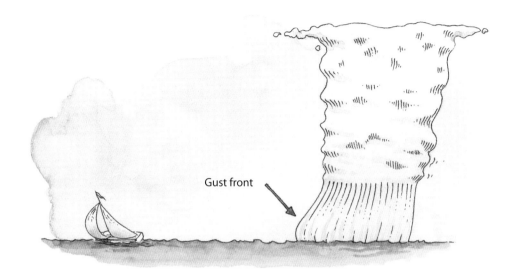

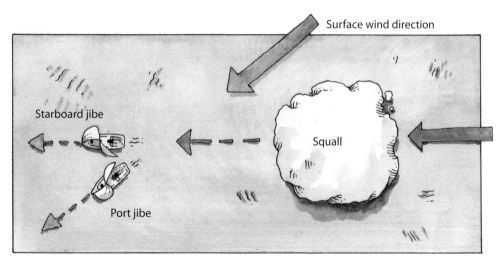

A port jibe is more likely to take you away from the path of the squall (in the Northern Hemisphere). (Christopher Hoyt)

has been slowed and backed by friction. A port jibe will therefore take us away from the track of the squall while starboard will keep us on a similar track (see illustration). Taking a bearing with a hand-bearing compass is useful to determine whether or not we are on a converging course with a squall. Alternatively, boats with radar can monitor the squall's progress on the screen.

As tropical waters are also likely hurricane waters, any sudden fall in the barometric pressure should be treated with respect and weather forecasts closely monitored.

EASTERLY WAVES

Sometimes found in the trade winds, *easterly waves* are shallow troughs of lower pressure moving westward at between 10 and 20 knots. There is generally fair weather ahead of the trough and cloudy and squally weather behind. The wind follows the arrows shown in the diagram. Easterly waves are most likely during the hurricane season.

DOLDRUMS—ITCZ

The *doldrums* is a band where the northeast and southeast trade winds meet—hence the name Intertropical Convergence Zone (ITCZ). As with all surface convergence, this gives a general rising of air, lower surface pressure, and rain, usually in the form of huge squalls.

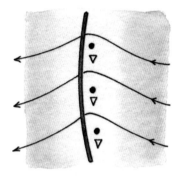

An easterly wave.

Doldrums. (Bluegreen Pictures)

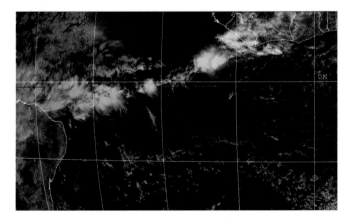

The ITCZ clearly seen from a satellite photo. This picture was for the mid-Northern Hemisphere in winter, when the ITCZ is at a southerly point. (NOAA)

This is the thermal equator of the world—moving north and south following the sun, but lagging by a couple of months. The mean position, however, is north of the equator. Over land the movement is much greater than over the sea bringing rainy seasons to tropical lands.

The weather in the ITCZ is usually one of calm, interrupted by vicious squalls and towering black clouds. The gusts can reach gale force with stinging rain.

It is not always like this; sometimes we have an easy transition from northeast to southeast trade winds with few squalls, but at other times a wide band of variables is met. It has been likened to a pot of water boiling; it's impossible to know where the next bubble is likely to break out.

Satellite pictures and computer models help in determining where the best crossing place is likely to be. The barometer is not much help as any changes in surface pressure are going to be small. The Coriolis force that spins the air around systems is too small at the equator to have effect, so the surface air tends to travel direct from high to low pressure.

Charts showing streamlines which give a better indication of wind direction than surface pressure charts can be found on the Internet. I have raced through the doldrums a number of times, and conditions varied from an almost seamless transition from one trade wind belt to another, to the frustrating flat calms and gale force squalls.

In the South Pacific there is an area termed the South Pacific Convergence Zone (SPCZ). This is a persistent elongated or sausage-shaped zone of low-level convergence that extends from 140E near the equator to about 120W at 30S. It is most active in the summer months (Southern Hemisphere summer); however it is closer to the ITCZ. In the winter months it is more transient and can affect the western side of the Pacific from near the Solomon Islands to Fiji, Samoa, Tonga, and farther southeast. The SPCZ is caused by convergence between the easterly trade winds near the equator and southeasterly trade winds from farther south. It is sometimes termed a monsoon trough, or trade wind convergence, and is similar to the ITCZ. It may be marked on synoptic charts.

There can be some strong winds generated if the SPCZ interacts with other systems.

MEDITERRANEAN WINDS

THE MISTRAL

The Mistral is one of the best known of the Mediterranean winds. The wind blows down the Rhône Valley with gale force ferocity and can affect a large percentage of the western Mediterranean.

THE BORA

The Bora is a cold and dry katabatic wind from the mountains. In winter, it reaches storm force and is reputed to have overturned trains! It can develop with little warning although the local fishermen will tell you that there is a marked drop in the depth of water before it arrives.

GREGALE

The Gregale is a strong northeast wind that is particularly important for sailors in Malta, where the main harbors are somewhat open to the northeast. This is mainly a winter wind when there is high pressure to the north, and low to the south.

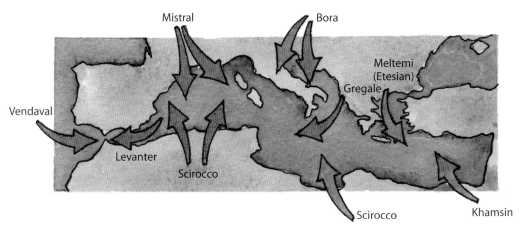

Some of the major Mediterranean winds.

Sailing in a Mistral near St. Tropez. (Bluegreen Pictures)

MELTEMI OR ETESIAN

The Meltemi is a thermal wind from a heat low developing over Turkey and Asia. It is funneled between Greece and Turkey and is strongest during summer afternoons.

SCIROCCO (SIROCCO) OR KHAMSIN

A southerly wind blowing off the deserts of North Africa is called the Scirocco, although it has many local names. It is a hot and dry wind that carries a lot of sand with it. By the time it reaches the north Mediterranean coast it has picked up a considerable amount of moisture and may well be accompanied by stratus clouds and light rain. Hated by charter crews, it deposits fine orange sand over pristine yachts.

THE LEVANTER AND VENDAVAL

The Levanter and the Vendaval are easterly and westerly winds funneled between southern Spain and Africa. The Levanter is generally moist and forms a banner cloud on the Rock of Gibraltar. If the wind is strong, violent eddies are likely around the Rock.

Local Winds

Every location has its local winds and pilot books are essential for gaining information about these winds. However, by looking at the topography it is possible to get a good idea of where strong winds are likely to be met. Local knowledge is important, and a good excuse for visiting the bar of the local yacht club!

OTHER WINDS

THE SOUTHERLY BUSTER

Rarely does a Sydney–Hobart race go by without a Southerly Buster. It begins with a sudden change in wind direction from northwest (usually) to south behind a cold front, and is usually accompanied by a sudden fall in temperature. The fall in temperature can be as much as 36°F (20°C). If the rise in pressure is quick, the southerly wind can be gale force and it is often marked by a crescent-shaped *roll cloud* and accompanied by thunder.

PAMPERO

The Pampero is similar to the Southerly Buster and found off the coast of Argentina and Uruguay. A line squall of high intensity, it separates warm and cold air at the rear of a low. A cigar-shaped roll cloud is seen on the approach of a Pampero accompanied by violent gusts of wind.

HARMATTAN

The Harmattan is an east or northeast wind found in northwest Africa. It is a dry hot wind, and coming from the Sahara; it can bring large quantities of sand out to sea, severely restricting visibility.

SOUTHERN HEMISPHERE

Most of our examples throughout the book have been aimed at the Northern Hemisphere, but when we move south of the equator many things reverse.

Probably the most famous cape in the world, this is Cape Horn on a good day. (Bluegreen Pictures)

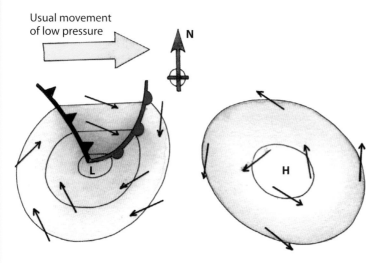

Usual movement of low pressure

N

Circulation around high and low pressure in the Southern Hemisphere.

In particular, the wind around high and low pressure is reversed in the Southern Hemisphere. That is, the wind around low pressure will circulate clockwise in the Southern Hemisphere and counterclockwise around high pressure.

The surface wind will still head in toward the low pressure and out from the high, so that the surface wind is veered from the isobars.

So, in the Southern Hemisphere, the greater the surface drag, the more the surface wind is veered.

Gusts are therefore likely to be backed by a few degrees, and lulls veered.

The sea breeze direction will also change; in the Northern Hemisphere a true sea breeze veers as the afternoon progresses, but in the Southern Hemisphere it will back. It may be difficult to reverse our thinking, but it is really only a problem for people sailing from one hemisphere to the other.

The equator is a band of low pressure and weather systems do not travel across it, but rather we sail out of one system and into another.

Backed and Veered

Backed is still a counterclockwise change in the wind direction, and veered is clockwise, no matter which hemisphere we sail in.

THE ROARING FORTIES

There are many stories from the days of the clipper ships to the modern round-the-world races about the *Roaring Forties* and the Furious Fifties. These terms refer to the weather found in these latitudes in the Southern Hemisphere.

The Southern Ocean is unique as the only ocean that girdles the world with no land to disrupt the flow of water and lows. Strong winds and high waves are the result and although the average wind direction is westerly in the Roaring Forties, in actuality the wind changes in direction quite significantly.

This is because there is a flow of deep lows that arrive from the west. Like the lows in the Northern Hemisphere they are made up of fronts with warm and cold sectors: the main difference is that the wind around these Southern Hemisphere lows travels in a clockwise direction. It is the seemingly continual flow of these lows that gives the area such a fearsome reputation. Between the lows are ridges of high pressure that may last for a few hours or a couple of days.

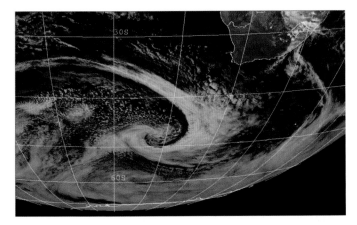

A Southern Ocean storm captured by satellite. (NOAA)

CHAPTER 15

Climate Change

Few days go by without a reference in the media to climate change or global warming. There is a consensus among scientists that global warming is actually happening and that it will affect people in both hemispheres.

Climate is a synthesis of day-to-day weather values. It is more than just an averaging of conditions as it not only takes into account average values, but also extremes, ranges, and frequencies.

We can think of the climate of an area as the conditions that dictate our overall wardrobe, while weather dictates what we wear on a particular day. In a sailing sense, the boat you buy and the sails you equip it with depend on the climate, but which jib to hoist and how many reefs to put in depend on the day's weather. There will always be a great deal of variability with the weather; some years will be warmer than others, some colder, but our averages, if everything is in equilibrium, should remain the same.

The accompanying illustration shows a simplified earth in equilibrium, with the amount of energy and heat coming from the sun equal to the amount of radiation being given off by the earth and being lost to space. It is, however, important to identify the different radiation being received by the earth and that being emitted. Short-wave radiation comes from the sun; some will be reflected from the earth's atmosphere, particularly by ice, snow, or water but most, around 70 percent, reaches the surface and is absorbed. What is of particular importance is that the atmosphere is, for the most part, transparent to this radiation.

The land or sea then radiates infrared (long-wave) radiation back into space. However not all of this radiation leaves the planet, as water vapor in clouds and other gases in the atmosphere absorb this heat and in turn radiate it in all directions. Our atmosphere works like a blanket, keeping some of this heat in; this is the so-called greenhouse effect and without it the earth would be a much colder place, somewhere in the region of 54°F (33°C) colder and life "as we know it" would not be possible. In local terms, when we have a beautiful

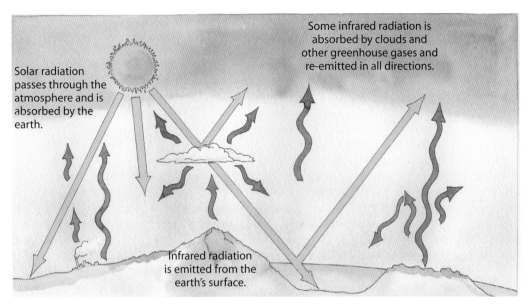

Solar radiation passes through the atmosphere and is absorbed by the earth.

Some infrared radiation is absorbed by clouds and other greenhouse gases and re-emitted in all directions.

Infrared radiation is emitted from the earth's surface.

When the earth's climate is at temperature equilibrium, internal and external sources of heat are balanced by dissipation of heat through the atmosphere and into space.

clear night with stars visible, the temperature quickly drops and this may produce frosts in the north. If however there is thick cloud cover, the difference between daytime and night-time temperatures is considerably less.

When incoming and outgoing radiation are in balance everything is in equilibrium. The problem facing us, however, is that gases put into the atmosphere by the activities of humans are causing an enhanced greenhouse effect and, as a result, we are seeing global temperatures rising at an alarming rate. The atmosphere is absorbing more outgoing radiation and re-emitting it to the earth. This phenomenon is widely attributed to the release of carbon dioxide into the atmosphere from the burning of fossil fuels, along with the release of other gases through industrial processes.

Throughout history there have been large swings in the earth's climate, from ice ages to periods when the earth was largely ice-free. Much of this has been attributed to variations in the earth's orbit and is known as the Milankovitch theory. As the earth revolves around the sun, there are three cyclic movements that combine to give different amounts of solar radiation reaching the earth. These changes occur over thousands or hundreds of thousands of years and in part explain our changes in climate. The difference in mean world temperature between extreme conditions is estimated at around 15°F (8°C) with the range being greater in high latitudes (the last 100 years have seen global temperatures rise by 1°F [0.6°C]).

However we are seeing an increase in global temperatures that has a high degree of correlation with the growth of industrialization and the increasing levels of greenhouse gases in the atmosphere.

HOW IS THIS LIKELY TO AFFECT US?

As the effects are not all fully understood, there is no great certainty as to the size of the effects; however, most climate scientists do agree on the principles. It is not as simple as it may at first seem, as many changes have a heating and cooling aspect to the change, making feedback difficult to quantify. For example, a warmer sea and air will increase cloud cover. On one hand the extra cloud will reflect some radiation, but on the other will increase the greenhouse effect. Taking both into account, this will have a net heating effect.

While there will continue to be arguments about how much the earth has heated, the topic of carbon emissions has become a political issue; the Intergovernmental Panel on Climate Change reports make disturbing reading. These reports are based on computer models, which are being continually refined.

Among other anticipated effects, a continuing rise in sea levels is expected. This is from the thermal expansion of the oceans and also from the reduction in ice in the Northern Hemisphere. Ironically the thickness of snow and ice may increase in Antarctica as warmer temperatures lead to an increase in precipitation.

There is likely to be an increase in tropical cyclone peak wind and rain intensities. In some circles it is thought that an increase in seawater temperatures, one of the criteria for tropical cyclone formation, may also lead to an increase in the number of storms. The year 2004 brought what is thought to be the first tropical storm in the South Atlantic (see photo), an area that until then had been thought to be free of tropical storms.

Generally, the weather is expected to become more extreme with more droughts and intense precipitation events. Classifying storminess is difficult, and although there could well be increased storminess, it is difficult to measure or predict. Although there is no real evidence

The Southern Atlantic is not considered to be in the tropical storm belt; one, however, seen here off the coast of Brazil, developed in 2004. (NASA/GSFC MODIS Rapid Response Project)

to show change in the expected pattern of the El Niño cycle (see below), global warming is likely to lead to greater floods and droughts that occur with El Niño events in different regions.

Over the next 100 years it is expected that there will be a weakening of the ocean thermohaline circulation. This is the part of the ocean current that is driven by changes in water density; temperature (thermo) and salinity (haline) control the density of the water. Changes in either are therefore likely to affect ocean currents.

There is a general circulation of ocean currents around the world that helps distribute heat from the equatorial regions to higher latitudes. While we are familiar with warm ocean currents like the Gulf Stream bringing warm water north, there are also deepwater currents taking cold water back to the equator to balance the system. An increase in global temperatures is expected to weaken these currents, and as they link all the oceans it will have a global effect. There is concern in Europe that the melting of Arctic ice will "turn off" or weaken the easterly part of the Gulf Stream known as the North Atlantic Drift. If this were to be the case, the effects of global warming in parts of Europe would be for temperatures to fall as the moderating effect of the warm water would be reduced.

Global warming is therefore likely to have an effect on boating as we have slightly more extreme weather events. This may result in bigger storms, possibly more frequent hurricanes, but we will continue to have interannual variability in our weather, with sometimes colder than usual summers as well as warmer than average winters.

EL NIÑO AND LA NIÑA (EL NIÑO SOUTHERN OSCILLATION OR ENSO)

Seesawing patterns of warmer water in the Pacific Ocean followed by a period of colder water were first noticed by Peruvian fishermen. This oscillation affects the weather over a large area of the world bringing droughts and floods to different areas.

El Niño means the Child or Christ Child in Spanish and refers to a warm water current that usually occurs around Christmas. The warm water replaces the cold nutrient-rich waters and fishermen see a sharp reduction in their catch; this is a small version of what we now refer to as an El Niño or ENSO event that continues for many months or years. The opposite of El Niño is La Niña and results in a cooling of the Pacific.

Under normal conditions the trade winds in the tropical Pacific blow from the east toward the west. These easterly winds blow the warm surface water westward so that the sea surface is about ½ meter higher on the west side than on the east side near Ecuador. This creates an upwelling of colder, nutrient-rich water, near the Ecuador/Peru coast that supports the local fishing fleet. This also means that there is a sea surface temperature difference of around 14°F (8°C) between the west and east sides of the Pacific. The warmer water on the western side causes convection and a greater rainfall to the west.

If the trade winds reduce or fail in the western Pacific, the upwelling in the east reduces and warmer water moves eastward. Along with the warmer water, convection is increased and rainfall increases.

Although this may seem like a local or regional phenomenon, due to the ocean and atmosphere interaction the temperature of the Pacific has global effects. Changes in weather patterns extend around the world causing floods and droughts. In a strong ENSO event we are likely to have warm winters in the northwest extending to Alaska, as well as above average temperatures in the northeast. Heavy rains are likely through the southern states resulting in floods and damage. The largest changes from the average are through the winter months.

Sailors in the Pacific will experience a weakening of the trade winds during an El Niño year and the ITCZ (doldrums) tends to move north. However, tropical cyclones are found to be more active in the east Pacific (a slight increase in numbers and an increase in intensity) and less in the west, while in the Atlantic, hurricanes are reduced in number and intensity.

Following an ENSO event the trade winds return to normal. Exceptionally strong trade winds can move cool water from the eastern to the central Pacific. This keeps the rainy weather to the west and the Pacific moves into a cooler than normal scenario known as La Niña (the Girl Child). Conditions tend to be the opposite of warm episodes with cold and wet winters in the northwest, while southern states stay warm and dry.

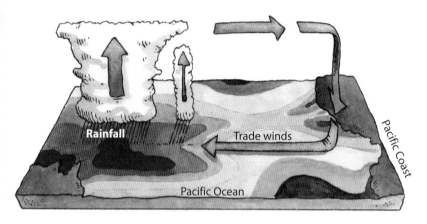

"Normal" conditions—trade winds are easterly, upwelling keeps the eastern waters of the Pacific cool; rainfall occurs on the western side of the Pacific. (Christopher Hoyt)

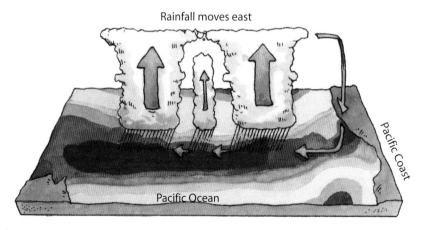

Conditions during El Niño—warmer water has built up and moves east, moving the normal band of rain east. (Christopher Hoyt)

B oaters can download weather briefing packages from the Natational Weather Service website (look at the radiofax section, for example: http://weather.noaa.gov/fax/masth.shtml for Boston, MA). The following pages show an example for the northwest Atlantic Ocean.

Briefing packages provide comprehensive forecasts for oceans extending out 96 hours, and are quite valuable when preparing for ocean passages. They include surface analysis charts and forecasts as well as 500mb charts (upper-air charts) and wave height forecasts. Be aware of the mix of units on the wave charts—some charts give heights in feet, and some in meters. (All art shown here is courtesy National Weather Service.)

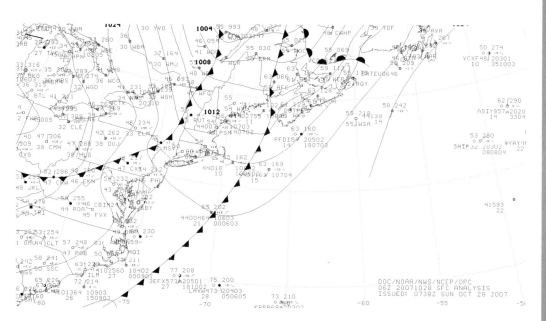

SFC analysis chart: this surface chart is for the same day and region as given in the left-hand portion of the surface analysis chart that follows. This shows the actual reports in the form of station circles (see page 13).

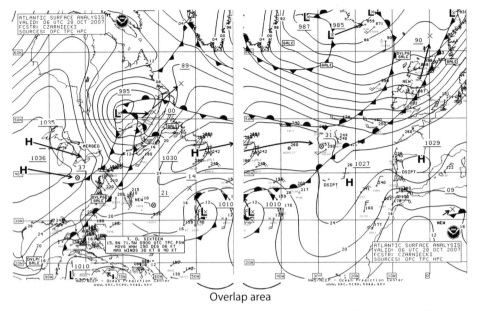

Overlap area

Surface analysis charts: these surface charts for the Atlantic are issued in two parts, with 10 degrees latitude of overlap.

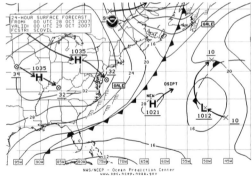

24-hour forecast.

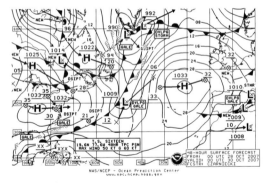

48-hour forecast.

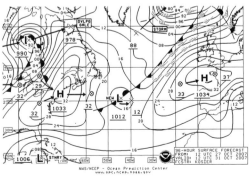

96-hour forecast.

Surface forecast charts: these are provided for three time periods—24, 48, and 96 hours. Note they are each prepared by a different forecaster (the name of the forecaster is found at the bottom of the title block).

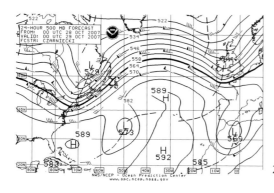

500mb charts: these upper-air charts are available as analysis charts, and as 24-, 36-, 48-, and 96-hour forecasts.

24-hour forecast.

36-hour forecast.

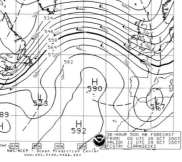

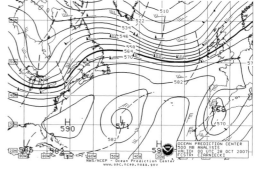

500mb chart.

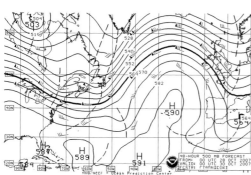

48-hour forecast.

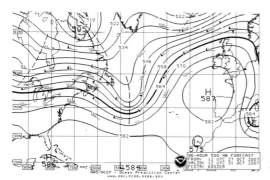

96-hour forecast.

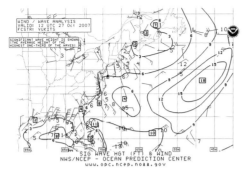

Wind and wave analysis chart.

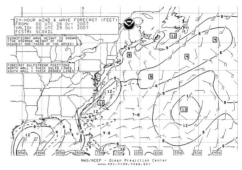

24-hour wind and wave.

Wind and wave charts: an analysis chart for the wind and wave conditions and several forecast charts (again in 24-, 48-, and 96-hour increments) are provided. (Note some of these charts show wave period and ice accretion.)

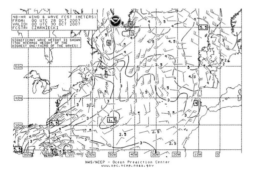

48-hour wind and wave.

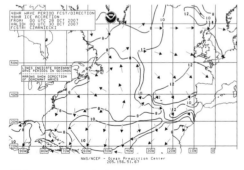

48-hour wave period.

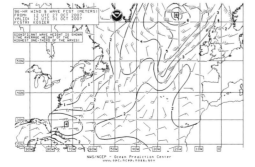

48-hour wind and wave.

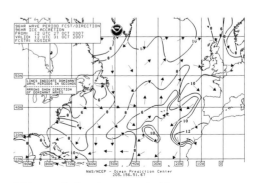

96-hour wind and wave period forecast.

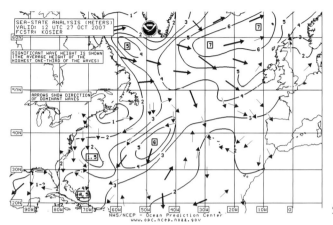

Sea-state analysis.

Other charts provided: also included in the briefing packages are a sea-state analysis chart, a satellite photo, and a tropical cyclone chart.

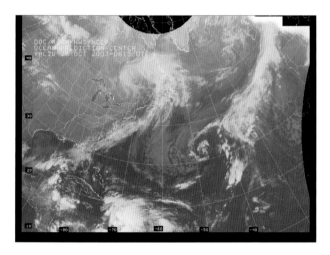

Satellite photo.

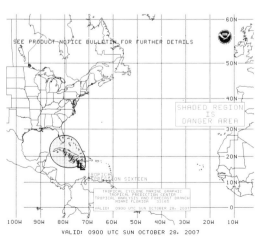

VALID: 0900 UTC SUN OCTOBER 28, 2007

Tropical cyclone chart.

http://www.nws.noaa.gov/om/marine/home.htm
The National Weather Service Marine Forecasts home page. With the forecasts and links it is the only site you really need.

http://www.opc.ncep.noaa.gov/
Ocean Prediction Center is also linked from the NWS site, synoptic charts and forecasts for the Atlantic and Pacific.

http://www.nhc.noaa.gov/
National Hurricane Center essential when sailing in the tropics and during the hurricane season.

http://www.nrlmry.navy.mil/sat_products.html
Great satellite pictures including satellite pictures with weather model overlays.

http://www.ghcc.msfc.nasa.gov/GOES
Interactive satellite pictures for anywhere in the world.

http://manati.wwb.noaa.gov/quikscat
Wind measured from satellites. Interesting to see what has been happening around the globe. Take care with the timing, as some of the data can be up to 22 hours old.

http://seaboard.ndbc.noaa.gov/
The National Data Buoy Center; buoy reports from around the U.S. and the world.

http://www.weatheroffice.gc.ca/marine/index_e.html
The marine section of Environment Canada site, providing forecasts for Canada and beyond. This is a good marine section. Note units are in metric.

http://www.nws.noaa.gov/om/marine/rfax.pdf
Worldwide marine radio facsimile broadcast schedules.

http://www.grib.us
A good source of Grib files. It has an added advantage of a free Grib viewer.

http://www.iwindsurf.com
A good commercial site aimed at windsurfers but also useful for coastal sailors.

It is possible to spend many hours surfing for good sites, although the information found is often the same, presented in different ways. Around the world, it is best to start with the local national meteorological service as many have websites and links.

Glossary

Advection fog. Fog formed by warm moist air passing over a cold sea.

Air mass. Air with little change in temperature or humidity over a large horizontal distance.

Aleutian low. Subpolar low pressure with an average position near the Aleutian Islands.

Anabatic. A wind that blows up a slope, the opposite of katabatic.

Anemometer. Instrument for measuring wind.

Anticyclone. An area of high pressure.

Anticyclonic gloom. When pollution, fog, and clouds are trapped by an inversion during an anticyclone.

Azores High. *See* Bermuda High

Backing. A counterclockwise swing in the wind direction.

Barometer. Instrument for measuring pressure.

Barograph. A recording barometer.

Bermuda High. Semipermanent high pressure that centers near the island of Bermuda.

Beaufort scale. Wind force scale from 0 (calm) to 12 (hurricane).

Blocking high. High pressure that diverts the usual tracks of lows.

Bomb. A very rapid fall in pressure as a low develops.

Boundary layer. The lowest level of the atmosphere where the surface has a big influence on the wind and weather. *See also* Marine Layer.

California Current. A cold water southerly flowing current on the West Coast.

Chinook wind. A warm dry wind on the cast side of the Rocky mountains, also known as a Foehn wind.

Climate. Typical weather conditions based on observations and records over a considerable period of time.

Cloud streets. Lines of cumulus clouds running parallel to the wind.

Cold front. The leading edge of a cold air mass replacing warmer air.

Condensation. When water vapor becomes a liquid.

Convection. The rising of heated surface air.

Convergence. A horizontal inflow of air.

Coriolis force. An apparent force caused by the spinning earth that deflects the wind to the right in the Northern Hemisphere and to the left in the Southern Hemisphere. Also called the Coriolis effect.

Cyclogenesis. The development of lows.

Cyclone. Low pressure or depression.

Depression. A low-pressure system, a cyclone.

147

Dew point. The temperature to which air must be cooled to become saturated and at which fog forms.

Diurnal. Daily.

Divergence. A horizontal outflow of air.

Doldrums. Low-pressure area near the equator with generally light winds but heavy squalls. *See* ITCZ.

Doppler radar. Radar that measures rainfall.

Drizzle. Very small water droplets that fall slowly and reduce visibility.

Easterly wave. A disturbance in the trade winds that can occasionally turn into tropical storms. Also known as tropical waves.

Eddy. A departure from the main flow in either the air or water.

El Niño. Warming cycle in the Pacific.

ENSO. El Niño Southern Oscillation.

Eye. The clear center of a hurricane surrounded by the eye wall.

Fetch. The distance the wind blows over open water.

Fog. Surface cloud with restricted visibility. The official international definition is visibility of less than 3280 feet (1 kilometer). However the National Weather Service reports fog when visibility is restricted to 6 miles or less and dense fog as less than one-quarter of a mile.

Front. The zone between two air masses.

Frontogenesis. The formation or strengthening of a front.

Fujita scale. A scale of 1–5 to describe wind speed and destructive power of tornadoes.

Funnel cloud. A tornado or waterspout when the circulation has not reached the surface.

Geostrophic wind. The wind blowing parallel to isobars.

Gradient wind. The wind blowing parallel to curved isobars.

Gulf Stream. A warm water current that flows up the Eastern Seaboard of the U.S. before fanning out over the Atlantic toward Europe.

Gust. A short-lived increase in the wind.

Gust front. The leading edge of a violent downdraft from a thunderstorm or large squall.

Halo. A ring seen around the sun or moon created by the refraction of light by ice crystals.

Horse latitudes. Belts of light variable wind associated with subtropical anticyclones at about 30–35° latitude.

High. Anticyclone.

Humidity. A general term expressing the water content of the atmosphere.

Hurricane. Tropical cyclone, an intense tropical storm in which wind speeds exceed 64 knots.

Icelandic low. An area of low pressure on averaged low-pressure charts.

ITCZ (Intertropical Convergence Zone). Where the northeast trade winds of the Northern Hemisphere meet the southeast trades of the Southern Hemisphere. *See* doldrums.

Inversion. An increase in air temperature with height.

Isobars. A line on a weather map joining places of equal pressure.

Jet stream. Strong wind in a narrow band usually at around 30,000 feet.

Katabatic. A wind blowing down a slope. Usually cold, it can be strong.

Knot. One nautical mile per hour (approximately 1.15mph).

Lake breeze. A thermally driven wind blowing from a lake onto the land. *See* sea breeze.

Land breeze. A thermally driven wind blowing from the land to the sea at night; the opposite of a sea breeze.

La Niña. A cooling of the central Pacific.

Lapse rate. The rate at which the air usually cools with height.

Latent heat. The heat absorbed or released as water changes state by evaporation or condensation.

Lee waves. Stationary airwaves forming under certain conditions to the lee of a hill or mountain.

Lee troughing. A trough of low pressure forming in the lee of mountains.

Lenticular cloud. A lens-shaped cloud.

Mackerel sky. Cirrocumulus or altocumulus that looks a little like the scales of a mackerel and is usually a warning of an approaching low.

Mares tails. High wispy cirrus clouds.

Marine layer. The layer of air above the sea.

Mesoscale. The scale between large systems and localized weather. It includes local winds, thunderstorms, etc.

Millibar (mb). A measure of atmospheric pressure.

Mist. Internationally defined as poor visibility but better than 0.62 mile (1 kilometer).

Multicell storm. A group of thunderstorms traveling in a line.

Nocturnal jet. A strong narrow band of wind sometimes found above the boundary layer at night when an inversion has occurred.

Nor'easter. A storm on the eastern coast of the U.S. with winds from the northeast as a low passes to the south of New England.

Occluded front. When the cold front overtakes the warm front.

Orographic uplift. The forcing of air upward by the presence of high ground resulting in the formation of clouds and/or rain.

Okta. A system used to measure cloud cover in eighths.

Pacific High. Semipermanent area of high pressure over the Pacific.

Polar front. A front dividing warm tropical air from cold polar air.

Precipitation. Any form of water—rain, hail, or snow—that falls to the ground.

Pressure. The weight of the atmosphere at any given point. Expressed in millibars. Standard pressure is 1013.2mb.

Pressure gradient. The rate of change in pressure over distance. The closer the isobars the greater the pressure gradient and the stronger the wind.

Radiation fog. Produced when the cooling of the land drops the air temperature to below its dew point. A land fog that can drift out to sea.

Relative humidity. The proportion of water vapor in the air.

Roaring Forties. Strong westerly winds found between 40 and 50 degrees south.

Roll cloud. An elongated cloud sometimes found with a gust front or squall.

Saffir-Simpson scale. A 1–5 scale for measuring hurricane intensity.

Santa Ana wind. Strong warm dry wind from the desert.

Scud. Ragged fragments of low cloud moving rapidly below rain clouds.

Sea breeze. A thermally produced onshore wind during the late morning and afternoon.

Secondary low. A low-pressure area that develops near an existing low.

Sferics. Radio waves produced by lightning.

Shower. Precipitation from convective clouds.

Stability. The tendency for air to rise.

Storm surge. An increase in water depth due to storms, particularly hurricanes, that can cause widespread flooding.

Squeeze zone. An area between high and low pressure where the isobars are squeezed together and there is strong wind.

Synoptic. Large-scale weather systems.

Synoptic charts. Weather charts covering a wide geographical area showing large systems.

Tornado. An intense rotating column of air.

Trade winds. Steady winds in the tropics around the east and south sides (in the N Hemisphere) of the subtropical highs.

Triple point. Where cold, warm, and occluded fronts join.

Tropopause. The top of the troposphere.

Troposphere. The layer of the atmosphere from the surface to about 8 miles (12km) (depending on latitude).

Trough. A mini-front with generally cloudy and showery weather. Also see as "trof."

Veering. A clockwise swing in the wind direction.

Virga or fallstreaks. Precipitation falling from clouds that does not reach the surface.

Warm front. The leading edge of a warm air mass replacing a cooler air mass.

Waterspout. A small marine version of a tornado over the water.

Wind. The movement of air in relationship to the earth's surface.

Wind sheer. The change in direction and speed of the wind with height.

Meteorology has a mixture of units that have developed over the years. Different weather services have their favorite units and although research uses the more scientific SI units, practical meteorologists have stuck with the more traditional.

This has led to an odd mixture of units. It is not uncommon to have cloud heights described in feet or thousands of feet, visibility in meters, and wind speed in knots—all within one forecast!

Pressure. Pressure is generally given in millibars (mb) or hectopascals (hPa): 1mb is equal to 1hPa so these units are interchangeable. Older barometers may still show pressure in inches.

Conversion to Millibars (or Hectopascals)

inches	millibars
27	914
28	948
29	982
30	1016
31	1047

To convert inches of mercury to millibars, multiply by 33.86 or estimate from the table.

Temperature. Generally in the U.S. temperature is in Fahrenheit but traveling away from the U.S. temperatures will be given in Celsius, sometimes called centigrade. The conversion is °C = (°F–32) × 5/9.

The accompanying table may be easier to use.

Converting Celsius to Fahrenheit

°C	-10	−5	0	5	10	15	20	25	30	35	40
°F	14	23	32	41	50	59	68	77	86	95	104

Differences					
°C	1	2	3	4	5
°F	2	4	5	7	9

Speed. The knot is the most common unit for wind speed but some countries, particularly Scandinavia, are likely to give wind speed in meters per second. For all practical purposes, the conversion is to multiply meters per second by 2 to get knots as: 1 knot = 0.514 meter/second.

151

Numbers in **bold** indicate pages
with illustrations

A
advection fog, 83–85, **84**, 118, 120
air masses
  atmospheric stability, 7, 8,
    17–18, 60, 67, 75
  charted representation of, 1, **2**
  circulation in high-pressure
    systems, 5, **6**, **11**, 45–46, **134**
  circulation in low-pressure
    systems, 5, **6**, **11**, **25**, **134**, **135**
  heat and global circulation,
    4–5, **6**
  meeting of two, 7–8, **9**
  moisture and, 4, 20
  origin and characteristics of, **7**
  over land, 5
  over water, 5, 7
  water temperature and, 75
  wind lanes, 75–76
air pressure. *See also* barometers;
  high-pressure systems; low-
  pressure systems
  charted representation of, 10–**11**
  cold fronts, 38
  defined, 5
  measurement of, 10, 151
  pressure gradient, 10, 12, 47, 49,
    51
  standard surface pressure, 108,
    109
  upper-air charts, 108–10, **109**
air temperature
  Arctic hurricanes, 25
  atmospheric stability and, 60
  cloud development and, 17–18,
    20
  dew point, 14, 83, 85
  heat and global circulation, 4–5,
    6
  lapse rate, 20

ocean currents and, 74
thermal effects, 3, 60–**62**
in tropopause, 4
units of measurement, 151
wind chill and, 89–90
Alaska, 119
Alberta Lows, 124
Aleutian Low, **119**
alongshore wind, 59, 70
alto cloud classification, 15
altocumulus castellanus, 81
altocumulus clouds, **15**, 16
altostratus clouds, **16**, 31
anabatic winds, 67, 126
analysis charts, 1–**2**, 49, 106,
  141–42
anemometers, 56, 98
anticyclone, 46
anticyclonic gloom, 47, **48**
apparent wind, 98, 99
Arctic hurricanes, 25
atmosphere
  boundary layer, 11–**12**, 118–19
  moisture in, 4, 20
  stability of, 7, 8, 17–18, 60, 67,
    75
  tropopause, 4, **6**
atmospheric pressure. *See* air
  pressure
Azores High, **121**. *See also*
  Bermuda High

B
backing wind, **30**, 31, 33, 37, 38,
  134–35
banner cloud, **18**, 133
barometers. *See also* air pressure
  forecasting weather with, 77,
    92, 129
  low-pressure system readings,
    31–**32**, **33**–34, 35, 77
  readings, availability of, 54
  units of measurement, 10, 151

Beaufort, Francis, 56
Beaufort scale, 56–**57**
Bermuda High, **9**, **22**, **24**, 46, **121**,
  124
blocking high-pressure systems,
  46
bomb, 78, 110. *See also* secondary
  lows
Bora, 131, **132**
boundary layer, 11–**12**, 118–19
breaking waves, **86**, 87
broaching, **78**
buoy data, 106, **111**, 146
Buys Ballot, Christopher, **25**
Buys Ballot's Law, **25**, 95

C
California coast weather, 119–21,
  120
California Current, 74, 85, 118
Canadian Maritimes weather, 122
Canary Current, 121
Canary Islands, **71**
Cape Hatteras, North Carolina, 8,
  121
Cape Horn, **134**
Catalina Eddy, 120
Celsius-to-Fahrenheit conversion,
  151
Central Pacific Hurricane Center,
  102
Chesapeake Bay, 66, 81, 124
Chinook wind, 126
cirro cloud classification, 15
cirrocumulus clouds, **15**, 16
cirrostratus clouds, 16, **29**, 31
cirrus clouds, 14, 15, 16, **27**,
  30–31
clear skies, 20
cliffs, wind and, **69**, 70, **71**
climate
  changes in, 137
  defined, 4, 136

global warming, 96, 137–39, **138**
temperature equilibrium, 136–**37**
clouds
  atmospheric stability and, 17–18
  blowing, 128
  changes in, 20, 76
  charted representation of cloud cover, **13**
  cold fronts, 35–**36**, 37, 38
  convergence, 67, **69**, 70, **71**, 72, **125**–26
  depressions and, **3**
  development of, 14, **17–18**, 20
  height of, 15, 16, **19**
  high-pressure systems, 47
  lack of, 20
  low-pressure systems and, **3**, 14, 17, **27**–31, **33**, 35
  sea breezes and, 63–**65**
  sucking, 128
  thunderstorms, **80**, **81**
  types of, **15–17**
  weather information from, 14–15, 17–**19**, 20, 76
  wind movement and, 14, 60
coastal forecasts, 100, **101**–2, 113–14
coastlines. *See also* land
  affect on wind of, 3
  alongshore wind, 59, 70
  headlands, 70–72, **71**
  high pressure near, 47
  offshore wind, 59, 67, 68–70, **69**
  sea breezes (onshore wind), 24, 59, 62–67, **64**, **65**, **66**, 72, 117, 134–35
cold fronts
  barometric readings and, 38
  charted representation of, **13**
  clouds, 35–**36**, 37, 38
  conditions with passage of, **8**, 37–38
  low-pressure systems, 21–23, **22**, **27**, **28**, **33**
  lows, families of, 40–**41**
  occluded fronts, 21
  rain with, 35, 37, 38
  secondary lows, 41–43, **42**
  signs of approach of, 35–**36**
  speed of movement of, 33, 49
  wind, 37–38
cols, 10
convection, 17, 63, **64**
convergence, 67, **69**, **70**, **71**, 72, **125**–26

convergence zones, 67, **69**, **70**, **71**. *See also* Intertropical Convergence Zone (ITCZ)
conversion charts, 151
Coordinated Universal Time (UTC), 52
Coriolis force, 59
Cowes, England, 66
crosswind rule, 14
cumulonimbus clouds, 15, 16, 17, 18, **33**, 37, **81**
cumulus clouds
  characteristics of, 15, 16
  cold fronts, 37
  development of, **17**
  high-pressure systems, 47
  landfalls marked by, 18
  low-pressure systems, **27**, **28**, 30
  sea breezes and, 63–**65**
  wind lanes and, 75–76
currents, 74, **116**, 117, 139
cyclogenesis, 8–**9**, 78, 110

D

depressions. *See* low-pressure systems
dew point, 14, 83, 85
divergence, 67, **69**, **70**, 72, **125**
doldrums, **6**, **130**–31, 140
drizzle, 13, 101

E

East Coast weather, **121**–24
easterly waves, **130**
El Niño Southern Oscillation (ENSO), 121, 139–**40**
equator, 4–5, **6**, 135
Etesian, **132**
evening race, **117**

F

Fahrenheit-to-Celsius conversion, 151
fair weather clouds, **19**
fetch, 85
fish hooks (clouds), 30
Florida weather, 124
fog
  charted representation of, 13
  development of, 7, 118, 120, 122
  meteorological definition, 101
  types of, 83–85, **84**
forecasting weather. *See also* synoptic weather charts
  accuracy of, 1, 49, 98, 104
  charts that show, 1–**2**, 74

cloud changes and, 20, 76
computer-generated models for, 1
overlays for navigational charts, 103, 106, **115**, 116
receiving data and forecasts, 103–8, **105**, **107**
safety and, 3, 73, 98
software for, 106–7
types of forecasts, 100–103, **101**
verifying the forecast, **54**, 98, 108, 111
weather briefing package, 117, **141–45**
wind speed, 98
Freemantle Doctor, 62
fronts, 7, **9**, **11**. *See also* cold fronts; warm fronts
funneling effect from land, 67–68, **69**, 70–72, **71**, 125
Furious Fifties, 135

G

gales, **77**–78
Gale Warning, 103
geostrophic wind, 49, 51, 52
geostrophic wind speed calculator, 55, 56
geostrophic wind speed table, 51, 52
Gibraltar, Rock of, 133
Gibraltar, Strait of, 67
global warming, 96, 137–39, **138**
GMT (Greenwich Mean Time), 52
gradient wind, 52–53, **59**–60, 65–66
Grand Banks, 83, 85, 122
Great Lakes weather, 124
greenhouse effect, 136, 138
Greenwich Mean Time (GMT), 52
Gregale, 131, **132**
Grib files, 106–7, **115**, 116, 146
Gulf of Mexico, 124
Gulf Stream
  conditions in, **6**, 121–22, 124, 139
  crossing, **116**, 117
  cyclogenesis in, 8, 74, 122
  fog development, 83
gust fronts, 43
gusts, 53, **78**–79

H

hail, 13
halo, **29**, 31
Harmattan, 133
haze, 13

headlands, 70–**72**
heaped clouds, 17. *See also*
    cumulus clouds
heat, 4–**5**, **6**
heat lows, 23–25, **24**
hectopascals, 10, 151
high-pressure systems
    charted representation of, 1, **2**,
        10, **11**, **112**
    clouds with, 47
    conditions with, **45**, 46, 47–**48**
    development of, 5
    polar high, **6**
    squeeze zone, 47, **87–88**
    subtropical high, **6**
    types of, 46–**47**
    wind circulation in, 5, **6**, **11**,
        45–46, **134**
high seas forecasts, 76, 100,
    114–17, **115**, **116**
hooks, 30
horse latitude, **6**
humidity, 1, 5, 7, 74
Hurricane Katrina, 94
hurricanes, **91**
    advisories on, 102–3
    alternate names for, 91
    barometric readings and, 92, 129
    categories of, 94
    conditions with, 91, 92–**93**
    development of, 92–93
    El Niño and, 140
    global warming and, 96, **138**
    location of, 91, 121
    names for, 94
    sailing near, **94**–95
    season for, 92, 114
    tracking chart, **97**, **145**
    tracks of, **93**, **94–96**

I
Indian Monsoon, 25
inland sailing, **125–27**
inshore sailing, 113–14
Internet. *See also* websites
    access at sea, 116
    forecasts and data available on,
        100, 103–8, **105**, **107**, **141–145**
Intertropical Convergence Zone
    (ITCZ), **6**, **130**–31, 140
inversion, 47, **48**, 61–62
islands, wind and, 66–67, 71, **72**
isobars
    measuring space between, **51**
    as representation of pressure,
        10, **11**
    spacing of, standard, 12

spacing of and wind speed, 10,
    12, 47, 49, 51
squeeze zone, 47, **87–88**
wind speed measurements from,
    12, 49–56, **50**, **51**, **55**

J
jet stream, **6**, **9**, 26, 30, 118

K
katabatic winds, 67, 89, 126
Khamsin, **132**–33
knot, 151

L
Labrador Current, 83, 122
lake breezes, 62, 126
lakes, sailing on, **125–27**
land. *See also* coastlines
    air masses over, 5
    effect on wind, 3, 23, **24**, 58–72,
        88–89, 98, **125**–26, 131–33,
        132
    funneling effect from, 67–68,
        69, 70–72, **70**, 125
    heat capacity of, **5**
    mechanical effects, **59**–60, 67,
        125–26
    thermal effects, 3, 60–**62**
land breeze, 24
landfall, clouds and, **18**
La Niña, 139, 140
lapse rate, 20
latent heat, 4
latitude, geostrophic wind speed
    and, 51, 52
layer clouds, 15, 17, 18
lee depressions, 23, **24**
lee troughing, 23, **24**, 88–89
lee waves, 69
lenticular clouds, 69
Levanter, **132**, 133
lightning, 81–82
local forecasts, **2**, 14, **112**
local winds, 133
long-term forecasts, 73
low clouds, 14
low-pressure systems
    anatomy of, **28–29**
    bad weather from, 3, 25
    barometric readings for, 31–**32**,
        33–34, 35, 77
    bomb, 78, 110
    charted representation of, 1, **2**,
        10, **11**, 40, **112**
    clouds and, **3**, 14, 17, **27**–31, **33**,
        35

cold fronts and sectors, 21–23,
    22, **27**, **28**, **33**
development of, 8–**9**, 21, 26
families of lows, 40–**41**
movement of, 8, 49
non-frontal lows, 23–25, **24**
passage overhead, 40
passage to the south, 39–40
phases of, 21–23, **22**
polar front depressions, **6**
rain with, 31, 32, **33**, 35
sailor's rhyme for, 26
secondary lows, **22**, 41–43, **42**, 78
squeeze zone, 47, **87–88**
tracks of, 26, **27**
warm fronts and sectors, 21–23,
    22, **27–35**
wind circulation in, 5, **6**, **11**, **25**,
    134, **135**
lulls, 78

M
mackerel sky, **15**
mares tails, 14. *See also* cirrus
    clouds
marine layer, 118–19, 120
Mediterranean winds, 25, 89,
    131–33, **132**
Meltemi, 25, **132**
mesoscale meteorology, **2**, **112**
meters per second, 151
microscale forecasts, **2**, **112**
Mid-Atlantic States weather, **123**,
    124
millibars, 10, 151
mist, 13
Mistral, 89, 131, **132**
mobile phones, 108
moisture, 4, 20. *See also* rain
mountains, winds and, 23, **24**, 58,
    67, **69**, **88**–89, 126, 131, **132**

N
National Data Buoy Center, 106,
    146
National Hurricane Center, 97,
    146
National Weather Service (NWS),
    100, 103, 146
    weather briefing package, 117,
        141–45
navigation charts
    Pilot charts, 114, **115**
    weather overlays for, 103, 106,
        115, 116
New Zealand, 23
nimbostratus clouds, 15, 16, **33**

nimbus cloud classification, 15
NOAA Marine Forecasts, 104
nocturnal jet, 61
Nor'easters, 39–40, 122–24, **123**
North Atlantic Drift, **5**, 139
Northeast weather, 122–24, **123**
North Wall, 122

O
observations, 111
occluded fronts
  characteristics of, 21, 38–**39**
  charted representation of, **11**,
    13, 21, **22**
  development of, 21–23, **22**, 38
  rain with, 38
ocean currents, 74, **116**, 117, 139
ocean passages, 114–17, **115**,
  116
offshore forecasts, 76, 100,
  114–17, **115**, **116**
offshore wind, 59, 67, 68–70, **69**
onshore wind (sea breezes), 24,
  59, 62–67, **64**, **65**, **66**, 72,
  117, 134–35
orographic uplift, 17, 126

P
Pacific coast weather, 118–21,
  119, **120**
Pacific High, **24**, 46, 47, 85,
  118–20, **119**
Pacific Northwest weather, 119
Pacific Ocean, 139–**40**
Pampero, 133
Pilot charts, 114, **115**
Polar Continental air mass, **7**
polar front jet stream, **9**
polar fronts, **6**, **9**, 26
polar high, **6**, **9**, **22**
polar lows, 25
Polar Maritime air mass, **7**
pre-frontal trough (pre-frontal
  squall line), 43
pressure gradient, 10, 12, 47, 49,
  51

R
race, evening, **117**
radiation fog, **84**, 85
rain
  air masses and, 7
  charted representation of, 13
  cloud types and, 15, 16, 18, **19**
  cold fronts, 35, 37, 38
  length of rain event
    terminology, 18

low-pressure systems, 31, 32,
  33, 35
  nimbus cloud classification, 15
  occluded fronts, 38
  squalls, 43, **79**, 81, 128–**29**
  thunderstorms, 43, 79–82, **80**, **81**
  troughs, 43
  weather information from, 18
rain radar, 106
red skies, **3**
rhumb line route, 47
ridges, 10, **11**, 46–**47**
Roaring Forties, 135
Rocky Mountains, 23
roll cloud, 133
Rossby waves, **109**
Routing charts, 114, **115**

S
safety, forecasting weather and, 3,
  73, 98
Saffir-Simpson Scale, 94
sailing
  near hurricanes, **94**–95
  trip planning, 104–6, **105**,
    113–**17**
  weather routing, 73, 74–76, **75**,
    107, 114–16, **115**
sailing areas
  East Coast, **121**–24
  Great Lakes, 124
  inland sailing, **125**–27
  Mediterranean winds, 25, 89,
    131–33, **132**
  Pacific coast, 118–21, **119**, **120**
  Southern Hemisphere, 133–**35**
  trade-wind sailing, **74**, 128–31,
    129, **130**
  tropical sailing, 128–31, **129**,
    130
  variety of weather, 118
sailing forecasts, 100–103
Saint Helena High, 46
Santa Ana wind, 58
Santa Barbara Harbor, **120**
Santa Catalina Island, 120
satellite pictures, **105**, 106,
  111–12, **145**, 146
Scirocco, **132**–33
scud, 14, 31
sea
  air masses over, characteristics
    of, 5, 7
  heat capacity of, 4–**5**
  rise in level of, 138
  water temperature, **6**, 74–75,
    125–26, 138–**40**, 151

sea breezes (onshore wind), 24,
  59, 62–67, **64**, **65**, **66**, 72, 117,
  134–35
sea fog, 83–85, **84**
sea-state analysis chart, **145**
secondary lows, **22**, 41–43, **42**, 78
semipermanent highs, 46
sferics, 81
short-term forecasts, 73
shower, 13
Sirocco, **132**–33
Small Craft Advisory, 100, 103
snow, 13
South Atlantic High, 46
Southerly Buster, 133
Southern Hemisphere, 5, 25, 92,
  94, 95, 133–**35**
Southern Ocean, **135**
South Pacific Convergence Zone
  (SPCZ), 131
South Pacific High, 46
speed, measuring, 151
squall clouds, 79
squall line, 43, 79, 81
squalls, 13, 43, **79**, 128–**29**
squeeze zone, 47, **87**–88
stable atmospheric conditions, 8
stationary high-pressure systems,
  46
storm surge, 95
Storm Warning, 103
stratocumulus clouds, 16, 47
stratus clouds, 15, 16, **28**
subtropical high, **6**
surface wind, **12**, 52, 53, **59**–60
surface wind calculator, 53
Sydney–Hobart Race, 87, 133
synoptic weather charts
  analysis of, 74
  availability of, 73–74, 106–8,
    141–145
  clouds and, 14–15
  features shown on, 1, **2**, **112**
  surface weather depiction on,
    10–**11**, **99**
  symbols on, **13**
  upper-air charts, 106, 108–10,
    109, **143**
  wind speed measurements from,
    12, 49–56, **50**, **51**, **55**

T
Tax Day storm, **123**, 124
temperature. *See* air temperature;
  water temperature
thermal effects, 3, 60–**62**
thermal lows, 23–25, **24**

thunder, 81–82
thunderstorms, 13, 43, 79–82, **80**, **81**
tornado alley, 82
tornadoes, 82
trade winds, **6**, 128, 139–**40**
trade-wind sailing, **74**, 128–31, **129**, **130**
transient highs, 46–**47**
Transpac race, 47
trees, 126, **127**
triple point, 41, **42**, 43
Tropical Continental air mass, **7**
tropical cyclone chart, **145**
tropical disturbance, 93
tropical low, 93
Tropical Maritime air mass, **7**, **8**
Tropical Prediction Center, 102
tropical sailing, 128–31, **129**, **130**
tropical storm, 93, **138**
tropical storm advisories, 102–3
tropopause, 4, **6**
troughs
    charted representation of, 10, **11**, **13**, 43, **44**
    cold fronts, 38
    conditions with, 43
    development of, 43
    easterly waves, **130**
    rain with, 43
    squall line, 79
    TROWL (trough of warm air aloft), 38
    upper-air charts, **109**–10
TROWL (trough of warm air aloft), 38

U

upper-air charts, 106, 108–10, **109**, **143**
U.S. Coast Guard, 103
U.S. Navy, Fleet Numerical Meteorology and Oceanography Center, 104, **105**
UTC (Coordinated Universal Time), 52

V

veering wind, **30**, 33, 38, 134–35
Vendaval, **132**, 133
VHF-FM radios, 103, 127
visibility, 101. *See also* fog

W

warm fronts
    charted representation of, **13**
    clouds with, 17, **27**
    low-pressure systems, 21–23, **22**, **27**–35
    occluded fronts, 21
    secondary lows, 41–43, **42**
    speed of movement of, 32–33, 49
warnings, weather, 100, 103
waterspouts, 82–**83**
water temperature, **6**, 74–75, 125–26, 138–**40**, 151
waves, 85–87, **86**
weather briefing package, 117, **141**–**45**
weather data
    interpreting, 112–13
    types of, **99**–112
    units of measurement, 151
    websites, 104, 141, 146
weather defined, 4
weather fax, 103, 106, **141–145**
weather routing, 73, 74–76, **75**, 107, 114–16, **115**
weather variables, 1
websites
    hurricane tracking charts, 97
    weather, 104, 146
    weather briefing package, 141
wind
    apparent wind, 98, 99
    backing, **30**, 31, 33, 37, 38, 134–35
    barriers to, 126, **127**
    Beaufort scale, 56–**57**
    charted representation of, **13**
    circulation in high pressure, 5, **6**, **11**, 45–46, **134**
    circulation in low pressure, 5, **6**, **11**, **25**, **134**, **135**
    cliffs and, **69**, 70, **71**
    clouds and, 14, 60
    cold fronts, 37–38
    convergence, 67, **69**, **70**, **71**, 72, **125**–26
    development of patterns of, 5
    direction nomenclature, 56, 59
    divergence, 67, **69**, **70**, 72, **125**
    funneling effect from land, 67–68, **69**, 70–72, **71**, 125
    global circulation, 4–5, **6**
    gusts, 43, 53, **78**–79
    high-pressure systems, 5, **6**, **11**, 45–46, 47, 52
    land's effect on, 3, 23, **24**, 58–72, **88**–89, 98, **125**–26, 131–33, **132**
    low-pressure systems, **22**, 39–40, 52, 77–78
    Nor'easters, 39–40, 122–24, **123**
    over lakes, **125**–26
    secondary lows, 43, 78
    thermal effects, 60–**62**
    thermal lows and, 23–25
    troughs, 43
    veering, **30**, 33, 38, 134–35
    water temperature and, 125–26
    wind bands (lanes), **74**, **75**–76
wind and wave charts, **144**
wind arrows, **13**, 104, **107**
wind chill, 89–90
wind shadows, 126, **127**
wind speed
    estimating, 98
    falling barometer and, 31
    forecasting, 98
    isobars, distance between and, 12
    measuring from weather charts, 12, 49–56, **50**, **51**, **55**
    pressure gradient and, 10, 12, 47, 49, 51
    units for measuring, 151

Z

Zulu, 52